Letters To Your Best Self

Written by Mandy Ekat

Original Title: *Briefe für dein bestes Ich* translated by Jenny Wade

Copyright ©2021

All rights reserved.

Table of Contents

Acknowledgment i
About the Author ii
Preface iii
Letter 01 1
Letter 02 6
Letter 03 10
Letter 04 14
Letter 05 17
Letter 06 20
Letter 07 25
Letter 08 28
Letter 09 31
Letter 10 37
Letter 11 41
Letter 12 48
Letter 13 52
Letter 14 55
Letter 15 59
Letter 16 63
Letter 17 68
Letter 18 71
Letter 19 74
Letter 20 79
Letter 21 82
Letter 22 85
Letter 23 89
Letter 24 92
Letter 25 96

Letter 26	100
Letter 27	104
Letter 28	107
Letter 29	110
Letter 30	112
Letter 31	114
Letter 32	117
Letter 33	120
Letter 34	124
Letter 35	128
Letter 36	130
Letter 37	134
Letter 38	138
Letter 39	141
Letter 40	144
Letter 41	147
Letter 42	151
Letter 43	154
Letter 44	157
Letter 45	160
Letter 46	163
Letter 47	166
Letter 48	169
Letter 49	172
Letter 50	174
Letter 51	177
Letter 52	179

Acknowledgment

First of all, I would like to say a great big thank you to my husband Mathias, who loves our life as much as I do – and has no problem with me sharing it with the world. I love you my sunshine! A huge thank you also goes to my family who have always supported me in everything I do. I'm also very grateful to all my test readers for averting many a disaster with their sound and honest feedback. A special thanks goes to my long-time friends Myriam, Rita and Sonja, who have always encouraged me in all my endeavours and from whom I have learned so much. And then there's my English Club and all its members who never cease to inspire me – thank you. Last but not least, I would like to thank all the people who have been part of my life thus far and who have made me who I am today. A heartfelt thank you to you, my loved ones!

All my love, Mandy

About the Author

Mandy Ekat, née Gummerlich, lives with her family in beautiful Schleswig-Holstein, Germany. She works as a lecturer, consultant and author.
You can find more information about Mandy and her workshops at:
www.briefe-fuer-dein-bestes-ich.de.

Preface

Dear ladies,*

Thank you for purchasing this book and allowing me the opportunity to offer you some suggestions and inspiration to help you transform your life from simply 'good' to 'absolutely amazing'. To help you on your journey, I've written you 52 letters – one for each week of the year – each inviting you to explore certain areas of your life and to practise what you learn along the way.

The intention of this book is to inspire you and definitely not to make you think that you are in any way inadequate. Rather, it's a collection of experiences that have helped me to finally lead the life I have always dreamed of and, by sharing them, this book will hopefully show you how you can do the same.

Everyone is different, with different dreams and goals, but there is one thing we all have in common: we can all benefit from the wealth of each other's experiences.

Enjoy your journey.

* And gents too, although the book was primarily written for women.

Letter 01

Hi lovely,

Let me start by telling you a little story. Last week, I went to the cinema with a friend to see a film. As it was drawing to an end, there was a scene which suddenly took me back to a situation from my own past – one I could really identify with. Here's a quick recap so you understand where I'm coming from. In the film, the main character had dropped a bombshell on her fiancé the night before by announcing that she no longer wanted to marry him. In this particular scene, she was throwing out all of the flowers he had sent her, which until the fateful night before, had been a bunch of roses every single day. After she had thrown out the last of the bouquets, returning to a room now completely cleared of flowers, I could tell that a huge burden had been lifted from her shoulders (a tremendous piece of acting, by the way).

There was a time in my life when I felt exactly like that character in the movie. In my case, I was already married when I announced to my then husband that our marriage was over. 'I don't want to be your wife anymore.' Eight little words. Taken separately, they are perfectly harmless. In this case, however, they brought a world crashing down for one person – but for the other one, it was the beginning of long sought-after freedom.

Eight little words that changed our world. It took a lot for me to say them, it certainly wasn't easy. There were our two families that had invested so much time and effort into our wedding a few years back. And what might other people say? But the worst part of it all? Having to bear that 'I told you so' look from my mother* – she had been right, the man wasn't 'the one', after all. So, what now? Could I bear the humiliation? Face being ridiculed? At night, my brain was in overdrive. My head wouldn't stop spinning, thoughts going round and round in circles. I felt sick. What was I supposed to do? It's true that I wasn't happy, but didn't other people have it a lot worse than me? Couldn't I just simply pull myself together and put up with it? It wasn't as if my husband was physically abusive towards me or anything. We just simply didn't click anymore, and the ongoing arguments were taking their toll on me.

But then came a conversation with my best friend and with it one of the most memorable light bulb moments of my life. She asked, 'If you and I were to trade places right now, what advice would you give me?' Boom, there was my answer!

Although we know the answers to most of our questions instinctively, it seems like we always need somebody to reassure us.

So, hear it from me now, lovely one:

You have the right to be happy and content – ALWAYS!

NOBODY has the right to force their will on you, give you a hard time, take advantage of you or treat you badly.

I'll let you into a little secret that will enable you to live the best life you could ever hope for:

You have to take 100% responsibility for your life!

Now, you might think that in a relationship it's more like 50/50. But, NO, it is not!!! YOU have to take 100% responsibility. YOU want a more intimate relationship? YOU have to take matters in hand and not only plan a romantic evening, but actually make it happen. YOU want to lose weight? Then it is YOUR responsibility to replace the unhealthy food in your home with healthy food. YOU want more time for yourself? Then YOU have to make sure chores are delegated and, if necessary, get some help.

If you wait around until other people change or learn how to read your mind, then, lovely, you are in for a big disappointment. It's not going to happen! Do YOU want to live a better life? Then it's up to YOU to make sure it happens!

If you think about it, it's quite liberating to know that YOU are the creator of YOUR life, that YOU are in the driver's seat, and that YOU only have to rely on YOURSELF.

Back to those eight difficult words. After I had finally said them out loud, it was as if a big weight had been lifted off my shoulders. I felt I could breathe again. Suddenly, I had the energy to take on whatever life might throw at me. And you know what? Nobody made a comment. My mother didn't give me the look I'd feared, and none of the other things that I was sure would happen, did happen. All of those nightmares and sleepless nights spent imagining the worst-case scenarios...

So, what about now? All these years later? Quite honestly, I could hug my former self for not waiting around till others changed – for taking 100% responsibility. My life might not be perfect, but it's amazing, nonetheless, and now I make sure that my future self will always have a reason to want to hug my present self.

Exercise:

Take a minute or two to really ponder the question: are you 100% satisfied with your life. Be honest! This is FOR and ABOUT YOU only. This is the starting point of your journey to an incredible YOU ... and it will also be a good reference to look back on to see where and who you were when you started and how much progress you have made along the way.

This exercise is step one towards your best self. You only know which direction to take when you know where your starting point is.

I'm really looking forward to accompanying you on your journey.

Take care of yourself, lovely – you are so worth it!!! Until next week,

Mandy

* By the way, I think my mother is the best mother in the world and she has only ever had my best interests at heart. I just wanted to make sure you knew that – so, you don't get me wrong!

Do something today that your **Future Self** will love you for.

Letter 02

Hi lovely,

I hope you had fun reading my first letter and some time to think about where you are at in your life right now.

As I mentioned before, you can only know which direction to take if you actually know where you are when you start your journey.

Let me illustrate what I mean. As the saying goes: 'All roads leadto Rome'. However, that would mean a Finn would have to travel south, a Libyan north, a Spaniard east, and a Bulgarian west.

Now, Rome might not be your dream destination, but an intimate marriage, a great family life, being physically fit, financial independence, four fantastic holidays a year or the freedom to do as you please whenever you want to just might be.

Still doesn't sound quite right for you? Would you be happy with simply being able to drink your coffee at home in the morning instead of on the go? With gradually being able to pay off your debts bit by bit? How about getting rid of that sinking feeling in the pit of your stomach every time you think of work? Or not yelling at the kids because life has you on your knees and it feels like you've been left to deal with everything on your own?

Or maybe it's the other way round. You don't actually know what you really want?

Have you simply been on auto pilot for the past few years, always hoping that you can somehow manage to do everything that is demanded and expected of you?

If so, I have just the right gift for you – I give you (drum roll) a genie in a bottle!!!

Yes, a genie ... and an exercise to go with it. Stop rolling your eyes, I PROMISE it will bring a smile to your face.

Now, just imagine that you are in the middle of clearing up, when you happen to stumble upon an old lamp – you give it a rub it and, hey presto, a genie appears.

Genie: 'Thank you for setting me free! You now have five minutes to wish for everything your heart desires!'

How do you feel right now? Are you nervous? Are you afraid that you have too many wishes or not enough? Or that others may find them ridiculous? Or that after those five minutes are over you can never wish for anything else ever again, so you need to make sure you get your wishes perfectly right?

Let me give you peace of mind. You can summon this genie as often as you want. You are allowed to wish for new or bigger things (set new and bigger goals) over and over again. Like most things in life, the first time is always the scariest and the hardest because you want to get everything right. But in this case, you can rest assured: there will always be a next time.

Exercise:

I hope you have fun with this exercise. You will need:

- a big piece of paper
- a pen
- a stopwatch
- and five minutes of your time.

So, now it's over to you: set the stopwatch and without thinking about what's actually possible in your life at the moment or in general, start jotting down a list of what you would love to have, see, be, or experience, etc. Don't go into too much detail, we will do that later on. You need to write down as much as you possibly can in those five minutes.

Just in case you need some inspiration or simply want to see what somebody else might wish for, here are a few examples I came up with:

- Trip to London with my husband at Christmas time, including a stay at a 5-star hotel
- Bathtub
- Gardener
- House for my parents
- Heated pool in the back garden
- Beautiful clothes
- Private language teacher
- New curtains for the bedroom
- Driving a quad bike

- Conservatory
- Regular massages and facial treatments
- Regular games nights with the kids
- Yoga room/study with super expensive luxury armchairs
- Golf cart
- New sideboards for the hallway

Those are just 15 of the 52 wishes I wrote down, when I did this exercise for the first time. And you know what? Many of those things on this list have already become reality, even though they felt far out of my reach at the time of writing. And I'm certain that the remaining wishes will also come true in due course!

Take care of yourself, lovely – you are so worth it!!! Until next week,

Mandy

You see things; you say, 'Why?' but I dream things that never were; and I say 'Why not?'

George Bernard Shaw

Letter 03

Hi lovely,

Did you enjoy writing down your goals and dreams? Or do you now feel overwhelmed and have no idea where to start? If this is the case, let me give you a tip. It really doesn't matter WHERE you start. The important thing is THAT you start!

When I started to look into personal development, I had a burning desire to change EVERYTHING for the better all AT ONCE. But I soon realized that it's impossible to do this. We are, after all, creatures of habit. For instance, if I'm used to drinking my tea in the morning with milk and sugar, as I have done for the past decade, I can hardly expect it to be as enjoyable if I leave out the sugar all of a sudden. The same is true for physical exercise. If I haven't done any for the past 20 years, I'm not going to start working out for an hour every day from one day to the next. Oh, and just because my head decides to sleep with my husband every day from now on, it doesn't mean that my mood or my body feels the same way about that idea.

Let's stop any negativity in its tracks – I've already managed to make some amazing changes in my life, but the changes didn't come overnight. In order to break a habit or establish a new one, ONE thing is absolutely essential:

T I M E!!!

So back to the story. Remember my list of 52 things? Well, once I'd written it, I had no idea where to begin. It was my mentor Darren Hardy who then made a simple suggestion: 'Just go for it! Take the first step and you'll be amazed at how incredible changes will just start happening.'

He was right. One of my goals was to drink more water. So, I started making sure that I always had a big glass of water with every meal and always took a bottle with me to the office. And, hey presto, after a couple of months, I wasn't thinking twice about drinking two to three liters of water a day.

I wanted to eat more healthily, but instead of trying out a radical new diet, I tried new healthy recipes here and there instead, cooking the ones I liked more often. Then I experimented with the ingredients to make it even more fun.

I vividly remember a situation at the supermarket a few months after I'd cooked my first healthy recipe. I was navigating my shopping trolley through the sweets section to buy a bar of dark chocolate. Crisps and the like where of no interest to me by then. My trolley was full of fruits and vegetables – not because I felt compelled to buy these things, but because I actually liked them. Anyway, there was a couple whose trolley was filled with all sorts of unhealthy items like fizzy drinks, snacks and ready meals. Needless to say, they weren't exactly a glowing picture of health. It reminded me that not that long ago, I was the one pushing a trolley with similar contents, feeling overweight and unhappy in my skin. I felt the overwhelming urge to call my husband right away to tell him how proud I was of myself for being able to make the shift from an unhealthy lifestyle to a healthier one, with the added bonus of finally losing a few excess pounds, having clearer skin and definitely a lot more energy. When I rang my husband, he told me that he was very proud of me too for sticking to my guns, which was music to my ears.

But remember, this transformation didn't happen overnight, it took months. And I'd be lying to you if I said I never ever eat any junk food anymore. The reason I wanted to tell you this story was not to use it as an opportunity to blow my own trumpet, but to encourage you to be proud of yourself and to celebrate all your successes, however big or small, as they are what make life so rewarding.

There is a proverb that sums it up: "The best time to plant a tree was twenty years ago, the second-best time is today!"

Just make a start! Think about the most important goal on your wish list to a better version of yourself and take the first step. Don't try to change everything at once – that's bound to end in failure. You'll only get frustrated if you try to tackle all of your goals at once. But if you see the first successes in one area of your life, it will keep you motivated to continue this journey to a better you.

Exercise:

Take a look at your wish list and sort the wishes into time categories, e.g. short term, medium term, long term, in the next 24 hours, in a month, this year, in a year, in the next five or ten years.

Take care of yourself, lovely – you are so worth it!!! Until next week,

Mandy

PS: Recently, I asked my husband if my face had somehow changed. It seemed to me it had when I looked in the mirror that night. He said that my facial features were more relaxed, because I don't see or judge everything as grimly or critically as I used to. I think I'll keep working on that one :-)

Time passes anyway
Make the best of it

Mandy Eka

Letter 04

Hi lovely,

I went to a gala at the weekend. All the dancers who took part in it were students from a ballet school, so not fully trained, professional dancers as yet. There was tap-dancing, jazz dance and, of course, classical ballet. Although the slender ballerinas looked very elegant and graceful in their tutus, I have to say that some of them had looks on their faces that made them come across as quite aloof. Well, that's how it seemed to me anyway.

Halfway through the show, they performed a dance which combined ballet and jazz, and one dancer in particular caught my attention. She was neither the slimmest nor the fattest, the smallest nor the tallest of the dancers. She didn't have fabulous hair or a remarkable face; in fact, she was just very 'average-looking'. HOWEVER, I only saw HER. Although the stage was full, it was as if she was dancing all by herself. This woman had incredible charisma. It was truly phenomenal. Her zest for life and pure pleasure in dancing left me spellbound.

It was exactly at that moment that I thought, 'That's it! You don't have to be the prettiest, tallest, slimmest person in a room to stand out or attract attention. It's not about wearing a stunning dress or make-up for a beautiful, flawless complexion. No, it's all about your attitude towards life.

When you smile, your eyes and whole being need to smile with you. You have to feel real joy in order to emanate it, otherwise you'd just be deceiving yourself, which is the worst kind of lie of all.

That reminds me of another instance. A few years ago, I visited my friend in Switzerland and one evening we decided to go out for dinner. I suggested going to the Italian restaurant we'd been to many years before when we were just 17 or 18 years old, and where we'd been served a pizza in the shape of a heart.

Before I continue, I'd just like to point out that my friend is a breathtakingly beautiful woman. Her mother is Swiss, and her father is Moroccan. She is tall and has long, black, curly hair, curves in all the right places and knows how to turn heads. And this friend said to me, 'Mandy, since that heart pizza, I've been back to that Italian restaurant so many times and have never been given one like it again. We were given it that time because of you!' I denied it vehemently, because with my weight problems and second-hand clothes at the time I didn't exactly embody the image of a dream woman who needed impressing with a heart-shaped pizza. But my friend insisted, 'You've always had a certain charisma. People feel comfortable with you and when you laugh, it always comes from the heart.'

You know what? She's right. I like people, and love getting to know new people. I'm truly interested in them and they feel that too. They open up to me and I can meet them with love because I have learned to love and accept myself for who I am. And that's exactly what the dancer emanated that weekend. She loved what she was doing and felt so infinitely comfortable in her own skin that she had us all under her spell.

You can do that too! Learn to love yourself, rough edges and all. You are special and unique. Don't allow yourself to be labelled by anyone, and don't feel like you have to change just to please others. Changes are only meaningful and necessary if YOU want them to happen to feel better in your own skin.

Exercise:
When you go to bed tonight, go through every part of your body in your mind and thank it for being part of you and making you who you are. Find something positive for every part of your body. For example, if you don't like your feet, you can still say, 'Thank you for carrying me through life.' Then promise your body that you will treat it with respect and love in the future, in whatever form that might take. Maybe you'll drink more water to flush out toxins or up your skin care regime, starting with moisturising those dry elbows. I know you'll think of something.

Take care of yourself lovely – you are so worth it!!! Until next week,

Mandy

Beauty begins the moment you decide to be yourself.

Coco Chanel

Letter 05

Hi lovely,

Today, I'd like to take the opportunity to write to you about criticism and gratitude.

What's the first thing you think of when you hear those two words in a sentence? Maybe something along the lines of: 'Why should I be grateful for someone telling me I've done something wrong? Do they think they know better than me? They have no idea! What gives them the right to criticise me? They're even less capable of managing their own affairs than I am!' Incidentally, that almost always used to be my first reaction to criticism – and, to be honest, it sometimes still is.

So, let's get started...

First of all, I would like to thank YOU not only for allowing me to accompany you, but also for accompanying me on this journey. Thank you for taking the time every week to read my letters and think about them. I welcome any kind of feedback – it's greatly appreciated! Please visit my website and leave your message at: www.Mandyekat.de. I'm well aware of the fact that I wouldn't be able to achieve my goals without the help of others, because I can't know everything. Also, tapping into other people's experiences, wishes, dreams and thoughts saves me from having to make all the mistakes myself and that's a huge bonus!

Obviously, I get feedback on things I do, which may be critical. And, yes, to be honest, it can hurt, but I'm usually the one who asked for the feedback!!! And obviously, I (still) don't exactly rejoice when someone tells me that my work isn't perfect, but as I write this letter, I also have to laugh. Of course, I'm not perfect. In fact, I stopped striving for perfection a long time ago as I believe there is no such thing. As we well know, there are as many ways to do something as there are people. And everyone has a different idea of what perfection is anyway.

I have a vision of how I want my life to be and in order to put it into practice, I still have to make improvements in certain areas of my life. That's why this maxim is right for me: ***I do not strive for perfection, but for improvement!***

I made my fair share of mistakes in the past when I thought I was too clever to listen to anybody else. But I'm glad to say I've become a little bit wiser with age.

Last week, a young woman came up to me and declared, 'I can't believe I'm saying this, but you were actually right. Why didn't I listen to you?' In response, I nearly said, 'Yes, you should have listened to me. It would have saved you a lot of tears and heartache.' But I didn't. Making your own mistakes is crucial and part and parcel of the self-development process.

However, it's incredibly difficult and takes a lot of practice to see criticism for what it really is: an opportunity for self-improvement and to make your life a better one for YOU.

Exercise:

Think about how you react to criticism. Then take your time to explore this a little further – could the critics be right? Now for your challenge: try to accept criticism. Are you able to use it to work on a better you and get one step closer to your dream life?

Take care of yourself, lovely – you are so worth it!!! Until next week,

Mandy

Critique is the prerequisite for improvement.

Georg-Wilhelm Exler

Letter 06

Hi lovely,

I have to admit that I'm a real personal development junkie, always on the lookout for new ways to further my personal growth. I've spent many an hour on YouTube and various websites, read tons of books and talked to all kinds of people. And I've always liked to believe that somewhere there is that ONE (elusive) FORMULA for success. But as is always the way, I read a book and feel totally inspired – and then enthusiastically attempt to put everything I've just read into practice. And the result? It turns out that it isn't entirely right for my life after all.

For example, below is my plan for a highly productive day where I manage to do absolutely EVERYTHING and everything goes perfectly (!!!):

5 a.m.: Get up, do 30 minutes of yoga, write my journal for 30 minutes, set goals, etc.

6 a.m.: Wake up the kids, go for a shower and have a nice, relaxed breakfast including a green smoothie.

7 a.m.: All the kids are on their way to school with a lunchbox full of well-balanced, healthy mid-morning snacks, and the little one goes to childcare with a cheerful smile so that I can get to work on time, not at all stressed out.

8 a.m. to 1 p.m.: At work. I don't get wound up, I'm the personification of calm (well, I did do yoga this morning!!!).

I tick off all my tasks without losing my cool once (after all, I'm committed to personal development and know for a fact that getting stressed or in a flap won't get me anywhere, it will just deplete me of my positive energy).

1 p.m.: All the kids are back home (those are the school hours here). We eat a lovely, healthy lunch together and catch up on everything going on at the moment.

3 p.m.: We go for a walk through the woods together and enjoy the fresh air, before returning home for some homemade cake and hot chocolate and to play a game or two.

5 p.m.: I use the hour before dinner to get my house in order. Obviously, this is brilliantly organized which means I'm highly efficient. I've even planned the meals for the day after and already bought all the ingredients I need.

6 p.m.: My husband gets back from work and we all eat dinner together – of course, everyone loves it!!!

7 p.m.: The kids get ready for bed on their own, the little one is read a bedtime story, and everyone gets a kiss goodnight.

8 p.m.: All the kids are in bed; the chores have been done. I had a minute to make myself look presentable and now my husband and I spend a little time together before going to bed for the most fantastic sex ever.

9 p.m.: My husband and I have read, talked, had sex and are now ready for those oh so important eight hours of sleep …
ZZZZZZ

And now that I've finished describing my 'perfect' day, I feel totally exhausted and fed up. I hate that feeling of constantly having to look at the clock and apart from anything else, there's no way that a day would ever work like that in our family. Why not? Because our life often has other plans in store. So, my plan might look great on paper, but in my world, there are so many things that just happen unexpectedly. I don't necessarily mean negative things like getting a cold or that test revision that refuses to stick in a teenager's brain; it could be an invitation somewhere, an unannounced visit or a flash of inspiration.

I have to smile while writing this as my little one, for example, really hates having to go to childcare every morning. I bear the brunt of the screaming and shouting, which means that far from being relaxed when I arrive at work, I often arrive torn with guilt.

My husband and I are both self-employed, so if we're lucky, we might get to bed at around 11–11.30 at night. And I don't think he has ever managed to get home regularly at a particular time. Our day has always long started by 6 a.m., but definitely not with yoga. I wouldn't be able to enjoy it anyway, because I'd be thinking the whole time, 'I hope I can finish this exercise before one of the kids turns up needing something from me.' (e.g. trip to the toilet, money for the class outing, a costume for World Book Day –

obviously, someone should have told me about this yesterday, but unfortunately that someone forgot!)

Recently I went for a walk through the woods, alone, because nobody wanted to come with me. As I was walking, I started to think about all the knowledge I'd collected over the years, how many things I'd tried to incorporate into our day-to-day life, and how much of this had actually improved things for us instead of just causing even more stress.

I think I've done quite a good job at cherry-picking the best parts and applying them to my life. I'm pretty certain I'm nowhere near the end of my journey yet, but it's still great to see how positively things are turning out. In another letter, I'll tell you about how I'm now able to do things that I used to think were impossible or far too complicated to achieve.

If there's one thing you should take from these letters, it's the knowledge that YOU in fact are the one directing your life. YOU are the one who has to weigh up all the options and try them out to see if there is something you can maybe do differently or better. It's very important not to let yourself be told what to do (e.g. yoga, green smoothies), but to have a closer look at yourself. Ask yourself these questions: What works for my life? What's important to me? What do I actually want to achieve? The ideal figure? Then exercise and green smoothies are probably not a bad idea. A harmonious family life? More time for me? So what if the neighbor achieves three times as much as you do – it's got little to do with productivity for productivity's sake, and everything to do with the areas where YOU want to be more effective so that YOU can live your dream life, so YOU can be happy.

Exercise:

Have a really good think about why you really want to work on your personal development. Is there a certain area in your life that you'd like to improve? And, if so, why? This why is the key! Take some time to try and understand why you want to improve/change things in your life. Is it because it's expected of you or because you have chosen to pursue a particular goal?

Take care of yourself, lovely – you are so worth it!!! Until next week,

Mandy

Life is what happens while you are busy making other plans!

John Lennon

Letter 07

Hi lovely,

I'm pretty sure, we've all been through this before: The day gets off to a crappy start, carries on pretty much in the same vein and then finishes as badly as it started. We can't wait till it's time to go to bed so we can write the day off and forget about it.

But does it really have to be this way? NO!!!

Fortunately, we have the power to change our actions, our attitudes and, ultimately, our lives in an instant. But how? By simply changing our way of thinking and accepting that the universe has something much better in store for us than what we originally had planned.

Here's an example:

I was set to fly to England to meet my host mother from Texas (in my teens, I'd spent a year there as an exchange student), who in turn was visiting her niece near Cambridge. Two days before I was due to depart, my husband called me to say he wouldn't be able to get back from the business trip he was on in time. My son was four years old and I obviously couldn't leave him at home on his own for four days. In a nutshell, I wasn't able to get my flight.

Needless to say, my first reaction was anger and disappointment. I'd been looking forward to the trip so much, not to mention the issue of the money I'd already shelled out for the plane tickets. But you know what – instead of letting the situation ruin my day or the entire week even, I thought to myself, well, it's only money after all. I can earn some more and book a flight for another time. I told my husband my thoughts and guess what! His company offered to pay for the next flight because it was the company's fault that he wasn't able to get home in time. As it turned out, the new travel dates coincided with the dates a friend of mine from Wales had booked as annual leave, which meant I was able to visit her too. Bonus!

There are two important lessons to be learnt here:

1. If I'd just accepted my fate and not flown at all, I would have missed out on a lot of wonderful conversations, experiences and excellent food. But since I know that I am 100% responsible for my life, I acted accordingly and found another way to travel.

2. If something doesn't work out the way I imagined it, I always assume that the universe has something much better in store for me. This automatically lifts my spirits, and I can act instead of feeling resigned. And just for the record: the universe has NEVER let me down!

Exercise:

If something doesn't work out this week as you had hoped, just assume (believe) that something much better will happen. This will automatically lift your spirits and you will find that you start attracting positive things into your life.

Take care of yourself, lovely – you are so worth it!!! Until next week,

Mandy

There are only two days in the year that nothing can be done. One is called yesterday and the other is called tomorrow.

Dalai Lama

Letter 08

Hi lovely,

Many people who work on their personal development do so because they want to make some kind of improvement in one or more areas of their lives. Productivity is often the main driving force behind this.

Sticking to this topic, let's begin a mini-series in which I will introduce you to some methods that have helped me to increase my productivity many times over without increasing my daily workload.

Today's topic is: FOCUS.

When I was at university, a fellow student once said to me, 'Mandy, never expect other people to be able to do what you can.' At first, I was a bit confused, because I'd always worked the way I did and assumed that was how everyone else did, too. Evidently, I was wrong! Now, this may sound a bit conceited, but it's simply the truth. I really do manage to get a lot more done than most people but that's all thanks to my 'superpower': FOCUS. When it comes down to it, I'm able to block everything out and concentrate solely on one task.

Sometimes, I lie in bed at night and can't get to sleep because I have so many things going through my mind. However, when these things really need doing, I'm able to stay completely focused and concentrate on doing just ONE thing at a time.

Here's an example:

I once had two lessons to prepare but couldn't see when and how to get them done. Suddenly, a window of opportunity presented itself in the form of fifteen uninterrupted minutes. Now, fifteen minutes really isn't a very long time, especially when you have to write your own text, think of a game to play and make something – not to mention, find two suitable poems for the language level in question. Needless to say, thanks to my superpower, I managed to get it all done.

The secret is that you really do have to focus. The moment you want to do a job quickly and well, you have to forget about the dishes that still need doing in the kitchen, the washing machine that is beeping and waiting to be emptied, or the phone call that is long overdue. Instead, you have to push everything out of your mind and concentrate solely on the task at hand.

What makes that a superpower? The answer is that not everyone is able to do it. But you and I can, because we have decided that we want to self-improve, become better versions of ourselves. Because we've thought at great length about what we want and how to achieve it. And when we set our mind to something, it happens.

At first, it's very difficult to truly focus, because there are so many wonderful distractions in life – which is why it's advisable to switch off your mobile phone so you can concentrate properly on the job at hand.

Make FOCUS your personal superpower and you will soon see what amazing things can be achieved super-fast when you set your mind to it.

Exercise:

Instead of trying to do five things at a time this week, concentrate on doing one thing first and then go on to the next. Needless to say, this doesn't mean that the dishwasher can't run at the same time as the washing machine while you check the fridge to make a shopping list. That's perfectly fine. However, if you have an important phone call to make or there's a conversation you need to have, remember to focus 100% on the person you are talking to and your topic to make it count for both of you.

Take care of yourself, lovely – you are so worth it!!! Until next week,

Mandy

> He who chases two rabbits, catches neither.
>
> Confucius

Letter 09

Hi lovely,

Does this ever happen to you? You get home from work, exhausted, and the only thing you really feel like doing is flopping on the sofa and relaxing. However, at home there always seems to be a never-ending list of jobs just waiting to be done. Quite often, these aren't even obvious, like the living room that needs tidying or the washing-up. It might be a box of photos that needs sorting out, a wardrobe that could do with a clear-out or that drawer in the bathroom that won't shut properly because of all the samples you keep stuffing in it.

On one such occasion, this was exactly the feeling I had when I got home. Although the house was pretty clean and tidy, it was still stressing me somehow. That's when I stumbled upon the audiobook The Life-Changing Magic of Tidying Up by the Japanese author Marie Kondo.

At this point, just a quick reminder – personal development is not about (re)discovering great pearls of wisdom that have been lost in the mists of time for thousands of years. It's actually more about looking at the world around you and at who is using which methods, before deciding whether they might be beneficial for your own life – or not. And the best way to find out? Just try them out.

That's exactly what I did with Marie Kondo's book – the examples she gave just spoke to me. I wanted to live that way too – without all of the things that burdened me more than they made me happy. I wanted my home to be a place where I could be efficient, where I could get all those everyday chores done, leaving me with as much time as possible to actually enjoy my life.

So, let's take a closer look at our mini-series theme of productivity. The KonMari method involves tidying up in a particular order that has to be followed. My first thought was, 'What a load of nonsense! I could do any of that right now, much faster!' But Marie is right. The order she specifies helps you to let go of things and reinvent how you think. Just like weight training to build up your muscles, you have to start with small weights first and then gradually work your way up. If you don't, you could tear a muscle, end up feeling exhausted, and be unable to continue.

This is the order to follow:

1. Clothes
- Tops, underclothes, dresses, sleepwear, jackets, belts, scarves, shoes, socks, underwear, sportswear, etc.
2. Books
- Recipe/cookbooks, novels, reference books, children's books, magazines, textbooks, telephone directories, etc.
Papers

- Recipes, user manuals, bills, receipts, birthday cards, handouts, workshop/seminar documents, etc.
3. Komono (a.k.a. miscellaneous items)
- DVDs, CDs, ornaments, tools, make-up, bedclothes, garden equipment, candles, vases, teas, crockery, toys, craft stuff, cables, medicine, straws, cutlery, plastic boxes, towels, baking utensils, etc.
4. Gifts and sentimental items
- Photos, personal letters, diaries, trophies, souvenirs, etc.

Marie's philosophy is if you pick up an item, it should spark joy; if not, get rid of it.

So, taking this on board, I began to work my way through it all. I literally had my hands on every single item in my entire house. Every fork, jar, medicine, book, sock, cable, newspaper article – you name it, I held it all. It took about four weeks, but the transformation was incredible. I disposed of forty large bags and boxes full of clothes and other items, and about two hundred books. And when I say 'disposed of' I don't mean I threw them out with the rubbish (although obviously I do throw away broken items or things that have gone out of date). In fact, I gave most things to the local charity shop. The arts and crafts stuff went to the childcare center and most of the English books were taken by the library.

Marie tells us to pick up an item and hold it for a moment. If it sparks joy, keep it. If it doesn't, thank it for being part of your life and then let it go. At first, that definitely sounds weird, but I honestly did find it easier to let go of things if I'd thanked them first. The thought of them bringing someone else joy instead of languishing in a drawer somewhere helped too.

Let's have a look at an example:

A few years ago, I brought two beautiful silk jackets back with me from a trip to Shanghai. I'd paid a lot of money for them and wore them a few times on special occasions. Now, they were just hanging in a cupboard. They didn't really fit me properly anymore, but what was I supposed to do with them? It was a real shame about the money and they really were beautiful. While I was on this mega decluttering trip, I decided to take them to choir practice and ask if anyone fancied having them. For two ladies, it was love at first sight. The red jacket was repurposed into gorgeous, eye-catching cushions. And the grey jacket has since been to the opera and graced special occasions. I'm so glad to have given my jackets a new lease of life and their new owners such joy. After all, I'd also loved those jackets and I was very grateful to them for that.

I found it particularly difficult to give away gifts, but Marie says that the whole purpose of a gift is fulfilled the moment it is given. Haven't we all received a gift that didn't really suit our taste at one time or another? The person giving you the present must have had something in mind when he or she chose to buy it for a maybe not insignificant amount of money, but I'm pretty sure it was never intended to be a 'burden'. Let the present bring a little joy to someone else by re-gifting it.

I also found it hard to give away books, but once I had the right mindset, it was the easiest thing in the world. After all, books are just printed paper and if you accidentally give away a book that you miss later, you can always buy it again. As for user manuals, just get rid of them. These days, you can find all the information you need online.

The first time I went upstairs after I had disposed of the books and looked at my now very empty bookcase, a wave of gratitude and relief came over me. The only books I now have on my bookshelves are ones that I truly love and take great pleasure in having, and in no way do they represent a 'burden'.

At the outset, I mentioned efficiency. That's one of the great incidental benefits of doing all this decluttering. You ultimately end up being surrounded only by the things that you love and actually need – and your cupboards and drawers are no longer stuffed to overflowing. Everything is a whole lot easier to find and you stop wasting precious time having to search for things.

I'll take care of the wardrobe next time. It's a story unto itself and a very different lady inspired me to tell it.

Exercise:

Have a really good look around your house. Do you love everything you are surrounded by? Or is it time to let go of stuff so you can breathe again more easily?

Take care of yourself, lovely – you are so worth it!!! Until next week,

Mandy

Letter 10

Hi lovely,

I bet you can identify with the following situation:

It's five to seven in the evening and you want to leave the house at seven. You are standing in front of your wardrobe (or in it if it's a walk-in), desperately waiting for inspiration, because although it's stuffed full of clothes, there's absolutely nothing – I repeat, nothing – you could possibly wear.

In this scenario, I can just hear what my husband would have to say: 'What do you mean, you have nothing to wear? Your wardrobe is bursting at the seams!' Men just don't get it. They get a t-shirt or a jumper out of the wardrobe, put it on, job done. When my husband packs, he needs about two minutes, if that.

This is what he does:

We're going away for five days. WITHOUT LOOKING (!!!) he gets out five pairs of socks, five pairs of underpants, five t-shirts, two jumpers, one shirt and two pairs of jeans from his wardrobe and packs it all in his suitcase. And he's good to go!

And me? What do I do? I stand there and think about it. I start to consider all kinds of unknowns! What if …? Or maybe red would be better? Those trousers are a bit tight, after all, and that top always makes me feel hot and bothered...

STOP!!! What on earth am I doing? How can my wardrobe be so full and yet, at the same time, so empty?

When I ask the universe something, it usually provides the answer – this time it came in the form of an American author called Jennifer L. Scott and her Madame Chic books.

One of the things Jennifer is known for is her TEDx Talk (YouTube), the ten-item wardrobe. Yep, you read that right: ten items of clothing. Well, that's one way of doing it, I thought to myself, whilst obviously remaining curious about how that could possibly work.

It should first be noted that such items as underwear, socks, sportswear, special evening attire, etc., fall under 'extras' and are not included in the ten items of clothing. (I have to admit I was somewhat relieved at hearing this :-))

Jennifer actually lives out this philosophy. Depending on the season, she has ten items of clothing that she rotates on a daily basis, combining them in different ways. The major advantage of all this is that you no longer waste time in the morning, or in our example in the evening, asking 'What shall I wear?' You will become very efficient in this respect, not only when you dress every day, but also when you pack your suitcase. The secret of the 'ten-item wardrobe' is to buy high-quality clothes that fit perfectly and combine well with the other pieces. Anything you don't like anymore, even if you once paid a lot of money for it, has to go. Anything that no longer fits, has holes in it or is worn out has to go too.

As with the KonMari method, you only surround yourself with things you love and things that make you look simply amazing.

The beauty of this (as with all things related to personal development) is that you can personalize it. It goes without saying that the wardrobe of a stay-at-home mum with two small children will probably look completely different from that of a woman building her career in finance. Personally, I'm still in the early stages of attempting to switch over from comfy mumsy clothing to comfy, yet more stylish, pieces. And what fun I'm having, too! It's not as if I have to buy an entirely new wardrobe straight away – I'm enjoying the process. At this point, it's each to their own in terms of taste. In summer, I prefer to wear dresses; I honestly don't possess a single pair of shorts! Some people claim they can't survive without shorts and t-shirts. And while some like clothing to be colorful, others prefer a more muted look. Some people like dots, some like stripes and others like checks. It doesn't have to be exactly ten pieces, it's the CONCEPT, not the NUMBER, that makes it interesting. It's about what makes you happy. Do you enjoy opening your wardrobe in the morning or are you overwhelmed or even frustrated by the sight of it?

Obviously, I can only speak for myself, but ever since I got rid of anything that was either no good or washed out or too small or too big, my wardrobe definitely has a lot more room and getting dressed in the morning has become a whole lot quicker. I wear my favorite items every day, instead of saving them for a special occasion. After all, we are all special by nature, so why not celebrate that every day? And if my favorite piece of clothing happens to wear out, I just buy myself something new.

Exercise:

Take a look in your wardrobe. Does it make you happy? If not, change it to make sure it does make you happy. Remember – take 100% responsibility! You deserve to feel good in your skin every day, and in your clothes. Wear the expensive perfume you got for Christmas every day if it makes you happy. Don't save it for that one special night. It was given to you to give you as much joy as possible.

Let's face it, when we feel good, we shine. And when we shine, we have the world at our feet.

Take care of yourself, lovely – you are so worth it!!! Until next week,

Mandy

Being perfectly well-dressed gives a feeling of tranquility that religion is powerless to bestow.

Ralph Waldo Emerson

Letter 11

Hi lovely,

This week's mini-series subject is meal preparation – i.e. preparing your kitchen and ingredients so that when it comes to actually doing the cooking, you're good to go with minimum effort involved.

In this day and age, an increasing number of people live on their own or are in a relationship where both partners work and have neither the time nor the inclination to spend two hours cooking every evening. As the main cook in our house, I find meal prep a great way to take the pressure off daily life during the week.

I don't know about you, but if I'm hungry, I'm a nightmare – at least, that's what my husband claims :-)

In order to avert an even greater disaster, it's up to me (remember the taking 100% responsibility thing) to be so well prepared that when hunger strikes it can be dealt with swiftly. And let me tell you, an empty or poorly stocked fridge is your number one enemy when it comes to fast, yet healthy, food. The same applies to the freezer, store cupboard and your lunchbox.

When it's time for a break, I have to have something to eat. That's just the way I am. I love eating and could spend the whole day happily munching away. My dentist once told me that I had very defined chewing muscles – hmm, I wonder where they came from?

Have you ever heard of bento boxes? If you google it, you'll see from the huge number of hits just how popular they are. These fantastic boxes have several different compartments and are originally from Japan. I love these boxes. Personally, I'd rather have a buffet than a set meal any day of the week, and that's exactly what these boxes allow me to do. I can make myself a small buffet selection with whatever takes my fancy – breaks are never boring!

Below are two examples of what I might put in my bento box, which has four large compartments.

- Wrap with soft cheese, ham and lettuce
- Cubes of cheese and grapes
- Pieces of apple
- Cashew nuts

OR

- Wholemeal bread with avocado and salmon
- Yoghurt
- Home-made carob balls
- Chickpea crisps

But I'm getting ahead of myself. I wanted to tell you first about meal prep in general.

At the weekends, I actually have the time to cook more elaborate dishes or entire menus. While something is simmering or cooking in the oven, I seize the chance to cut onions, rinse grapes, mash avocados, cut cheese into cubes, etc. This means that I can save myself a lot of time and effort during the week. I can just throw the grapes and cheese straight into my lunchbox or spread avocado on my bread without first having to remove the stone, spoon out the flesh and mash it with a fork.

There are many ways to prepare breakfast, lunch, dinner and snacks. Many a meal prep expert will indeed prepare all meals in advance and portion out all the snacks. This method eliminates the need to cook the food. It's simply a matter of heating it up.

I don't go as far as this as I usually have the time and inclination to cook every now and then during the week. My difficulty tends to be in the mornings, when I have a break during working hours and feel like eating a second or third breakfast. This is where my bento box comes into play. It simply makes my breaks more enjoyable (and making my life more enjoyable is the name of the game!). Some of my co-workers wonder how I manage to find the time in the mornings to make one of these lunchboxes not just for me, but for every single one of my family members. But I can tell you right now that with the right preparation, it's as quick as making a sandwich.

In this case, as with many other things, it's all about a mindset. I want us all to eat a wide variety of healthy food that keeps us going through the day in good spirits. And for me, that definitely includes a bit of chocolate!

I would never expect myself or anyone else to only ever eat home-made and super healthy food. Sometimes life's demands mean something quick is a must – and maybe requires just a smidgen of sugar. Alright, you got me: sometimes, m&m's are the only way forward :-) But I think that as long as I try to eat healthy food in general, that has to be a good thing. Now, there are umpteen different opinions about what it means to eat healthily. I'm not a nutritionist and I won't be elaborating on this topic. After all, our main topic is productivity.

So, if I know exactly where all my Tupperware, pots and pans, utensils, groceries, and other necessary items are, I won't waste any time looking for them. If I also know exactly what I want to cook when AND have all the ingredients at home, food preparation becomes a walk in the park.

Once a week, I take a good look at what I have left in the fridge and the pantry, before making myself a cup of tea and grabbing a piece of paper and a pen.

If food needs to be used up, then this is automatically integrated into the meal plan. Aside from that, I always need to have certain ingredients in the house to be able to make the bento boxes, smoothies or snacks. These include avocados, tortillas, cooked ham, pieces of cheese, grapes, apples, frozen fruit (for the smoothies), pasta, flour, milk and Nutella (obviously – the number one essential item in our house :-))

With time I learned what my family actually eats and how to best 'package' it. For instance, my children would never voluntarily eat an apple whole. But if I cut said apple – or for that matter, carrots or bananas – into bite-sized chunks, they will inhale them with delight as a snack or part of the bento box content.

If I stick to the plan, I actually save money, because I don't make any impulse buys and everything gets used up so it cuts down on waste. Even if I get an unexpected invitation to dinner, I can postpone the plan for a few days. What's more, I always have enough food to cover any surprise visits. It's no problem at all! My grandma used to say that soup can always be stretched with water. So, all I need to do is quickly whip up some chopped fruit to munch on in the meantime and there you go. Let's be honest, in the case of a spontaneous visit it's not so much about strictly sticking to a meal plan or about the food itself. It's about spending time in good company and creating wonderful memories. After all, a plan is just a plan. It's not designed to cause stress or show us what we can't do – it's simply a guide to help us navigate mealtimes and that's all.

On Fridays, we have our weekly film night when I use up whatever is left. I raid the fridge and turn the leftovers into finger food, which we eat together in front of the TV.

Below is an example weekly meal plan:

	Monday	Tuesday	Wednesday	Thursday	Friday
Breakfast	Smoothies/ cornflakes/ muesli/bread	Smoothies/ cornflakes/ muesli/bread	Smoothies/ cornflakes/ muesli/bread	Smoothies/ cornflakes/ muesli/bread	Smoothies/ cornflakes/ muesli/bread
Morning break	Bento box	Bento box	Bento box	Bento box	Bento box
Lunch	Pasta with salmon sauce	Tortellini with tomato sauce	Pancakes	Veg soup (Thermomix) and bread	BBQ leftovers
Snacks	Fruit/biscuits/ cake/waffles	Fruit/biscuits/ cake/waffles	Fruit/biscuits/ cake/waffles	Fruit/biscuits/ cake/waffles	Fruit/biscuits/ cake/waffles
Evening meal	Sandwiches/ leftovers from lunchtime or quesadillas	Sandwiches/ leftovers from lunchtime or quesadillas	Mexican evening, e.g. tacos	BBQ	Film night with finger food of leftovers

I don't tell the kids what to eat, but let them choose from what's on offer, and I make sure that we have everything we need at home.

The bento boxes could be prepared the night before, but I do this in the mornings. There are a few things I can do while having breakfast myself, but if the kids want to pack their boxes themselves, that's even better.

Exercise:

The suggestions and ideas can be adapted to suit your own eating habits and lifestyle. So, have a look and see if you can use some of them to make cooking easier during the week. Food should be enjoyed to the full and with all your senses. With this in mind, get prepping and bon appetite!

Take care of yourself, lovely – you are so worth it!!! Until next week,

Mandy

Food tastes best at a table set with love.

Letter 12

Hi lovely,

Your time is precious, don't let it slip through your fingers. Today I'd like to talk about time management and that time drainer, the one we're all guilty of now and then, PROCRASTINATION.

People often say to me, 'How do you manage to get everything done? I never have any time at all for ... (ANYTHING).'

To which I regularly answer, 'You have just as many hours in the day as anyone else – i.e. 24! It's just that you tend to prioritize the little things and ignore the ones that are actually important!'

This is generally met with a 'Yeah, but ...' Oh, how that drives me mad!!! Surely their problem is more to do with procrastinating?

I can't bear the constant moaning by people who think they either have to please everyone or simply want to, instead of focusing on what they really want. Society has clearly set us some kind of unwritten rules, otherwise there wouldn't be so many people complaining about not having enough time and about all the things they have to do, would there?

The thing is, when I actually question them a bit more about it, it often turns out that these people watch a lot of TV or are basically on social media all the time. Now, nobody is forcing them to spend their time doing this; they really are free to do whatever they want – so, should they really be complaining that they don't have time for anything else?

Let's have a look at a very simple example calculation. If someone watches the 8 p.m. film every night, which usually lasts around two hours, that makes 14 hours a week. 14 hours times 52 weeks is a total of 728 hours or 30 days a year!!! In other words, this person that ONLY spends two hours a day watching TV or surfing the internet, actually spends a WHOLE MONTH a year on this activity. Just let that sink in for a moment. This person spends a whole month of their life on the couch every year doing – well, what exactly? Getting educated? Working on personal development? Strengthening family ties? Improving their love life?

I certainly don't condemn television because I love movie night with the whole family. If anyone says they need two hours a day of TV to relax, please, each to their own. But then please don't grumble that there's no time for sports, cooking, appointments, the kids, partner, gardening or actual hobbies.

One disadvantage of television, which has nothing to do with time, is that it often seems to suggest things to us. Take advertising, for example. Essentially, every advert tells us that we are not perfect, that we are not enough, that we should look different, that we should dress another way. If we actually took all of that advertising messaging on board, we'd surely slip into a state of deep depression with the sudden painful realization of all our imperfections (in the eyes of the media). I don't wear that aftershave, so that's why I don't attract any women. I don't use that lipstick, so I won't get a raise, because my boss doesn't even notice me. My kids will end up in the gutter, because I won't buy them that toy, thus depriving them of the opportunity to develop into perfect little Einsteins.

I could go on like this forever, but it will just stress me out. You and I are unique and perfect just the way we are. We don't need things to make us perfect – it comes from within. Some people might say, 'I blame the ad agencies for making me feel so bad.' Let me put it this way: Nobody can make you feel that way unless YOU let them.

There used to be a kids' TV programme in the UK called Why Don't You? It's full title, though, was Why Don't You Just Switch Off Your Television Set and Go and Do Something Less Boring Instead?

Good question. We should switch off the TV more often and escape from the negative influence of advertising – and take more time for the things that are really important in our lives.

Exercise:

This week, write down PRECISELY how much time you spend in front of the TV and on social media channels. Then think about whether this is your way of putting things off, procrastinating. Could you be using this time more wisely? What would you do? Write it down.

Take care of yourself, lovely – you are so worth it!!! Until next week,

Mandy

Procrastination is like a credit card:
It's a lot of fun until you get the bill.

Christopher Parker

Letter 13

Hi lovely,

Have you ever heard the expression about loving someone 'warts and all'?

For the last few days, I haven't been able to stop thinking about that expression and what it means.

For some reason, I always seem to be on a quest for PERFECTION, to somehow be PERFECT while doing everything PERFECTLY. But then I get to a point where I have to make a decision, and ask myself what I'd rather be: PERFECT, but utterly frazzled? Or have a few 'warts', but fun along the way?

As PERFECTION is in the eye of the beholder, it's definitely a tricky thing to define. So, I decided to take stock of the situation.

Everything I do, I do with love. I always try to do the best I can at any given moment in time despite the everyday chaos we are all faced with at times.

Sometimes I get carried away, especially when it comes to organizing a party. Not only does the table have to be set just so, the house look like something out of a glossy magazine, and the food obviously of Michelin Star quality, but I most definitely have to look the glamorous part too. All of a sudden, I start running out of time, I get in a flap, and everything I'd imagined so beautifully in my mind's eye starts to go to pot. I break into a sweat, my hair starts to do its own thing, and my food is in danger of burning. So, what do I do now? Cry? Well, that won't do much good. My mum once gave me a great piece of advice: 'Go outside, shout "[expletive of choice]" three times and cry for a bit if you need to. Then come back in and figure it out, because life carries on regardless.' And she's so right about that. The people I invite into my home come to have a lovely time – not to judge me or disapprove of me. Unfortunately, I forget that sometimes. Luckily, though, I am surrounded by truly lovely people who remind me that everything I do is always done with love, and that makes me really glad. I feel honored that people love coming to my house and, to be honest, the most wonderful evenings are the ones when people just turn up unannounced.

As I mentioned before, my grandma taught me that you can always make your soup go further by adding some water; nearly everyone loves a simple bowl of pasta (no matter how fussy they seem to be), and a nice cup of tea always does wonders.

As far as cleaning the house goes, I really have to thank/admire my best friend for her infinite wisdom. She once said to me: 'You know what? Those cobwebs have been there for the last three weeks, but you only notice them just before the guests arrive. So, the guests would have to look at them for three weeks, too, before they even knew they were there.' Love that!!

When times are particularly stressful, like around Christmas, just before the big garden party or a birthday, I often think 'love yourself "warts and all"'. Then, breaking into a warm, friendly smile, I go and welcome my guests with a ladder in my tights, not a manicured nail in sight, and we have the most wonderful time ever.

Exercise:

Think back to the most fabulous parties, the greatest celebrations and the loveliest gatherings you've ever had the pleasure of being part of and take a moment to reminisce. Sometimes, we have to forget about the world and simply let our minds wander. Enjoy reliving those happy memories!

Take care of yourself, lovely – you are so worth it!!! Until next week,

Mandy

Love yourself, warts and all.

English saying

Letter 14

Hi lovely,

I had to laugh at myself recently. As you know by now, I really love to learn new things and more about myself and to get as much input as possible from many different sources. So, I was very happy when I heard that a new book by Denise Duffield-Thomas was about to hit the market. I've already devoured many of her books and audio books. She is a money mindset mentor for women and her mission is to help dispel old-fashioned ways of thinking about money through her books and workshops. She specifically focuses on women who are trying to make a career for themselves without a guilty conscience. Denise is married and has children, so her philosophy also draws on her own experiences in this role. As a married mother myself, it makes me appreciate her well-founded advice even more. After all, theory and practice can often be two completely different things. In any case, Denise, by her own admission, is lazy and always tries to take the path of least resistance. She gets help around the house and with childcare and only does the things she likes doing – and without any hint of a guilty conscience. For anything else, she pays someone to do it for her. As a self-made millionaire, she's living the dream – with kids and a career to boot. One thing she always emphasizes is that she is by no means super slim or always perfectly made-up. In fact, she loves her yoga trousers and really doesn't give a hoot about diets. From her point of view, none of this is important if you want to make money, because nobody can see you in your pyjamas when you're writing e-mails, anyway.

On the other hand, I'm a long-time fan of Darren Hardy, the former publisher and founding editor of SUCCESS magazine in the USA. He's a mentor and keynote speaker and, basically, the complete opposite of Denise. Although married, he has no children; he ALWAYS works hard (by which I mean that, unlike Denise, he doesn't take the path of least resistance) and, as he says of himself, he demands of the people around him that they steadily work on self-improvement as well.

However, Denise and Darren do have one thing in common: they are both millionaires and in their own way both want to help other people to live the lives they dream of.

As I said, I really like both of them. And the reason why I had to laugh was that both of them help me to move forward, even though their opinions are sometimes complete polar opposites.

Sometimes I have a Denise day where I take a totally relaxed approach to things and just go with the flow. I think about the things she has taught me, for example, that I don't have to do everything on my own. Or why would I think that I can only be a good housewife, mother and spouse if I do undertake everything on my own? It's okay to be a wife and mother AND be successful and earn loads of money.

On my Darren days – which actually predominate, because I love to be productive – I write lists, make plans, set deadlines and establish a structure for my life.

What I'm trying to tell you is that whilst there are many mentors, teachers, and speakers around, don't think that only one of them has the ultimate recipe for success, even if that's what everyone always seems to claim.

A dear friend of mine always likes to quote, 'There are as many ways to do things as there are people!' And that's so true! We're not all the same. Each and every one of us needs something different to make us happy or feel successful.

Let's take the morning routine for instance. One person may need coffee, another one a green smoothie, and someone else can never start the day without freshly squeezed orange juice. I love black tea with milk and sugar, personally. And who's the happiest of us now? All of us, in our own special way. That's what I keep trying to tell you. You are special and unique!!!

You don't have to become what others want you to be. You just have to be who YOU want to be.

My advice to you is this: If you feel the desire to change, listen to a lot of different advice. Let it sink in. Try it out. Look closely at the person giving the advice. And then make your own cocktail with a personal blend of ingredients.

Make sure it tastes good and doesn't give you a headache! Life is for living now, don't put it off until some point in time when you're 'far enough' down the path of self-development, as dictated by someone else. Oh no! Start living now and have a ball while you're at it, become a better person, more productive – if that's what you want. Because if you don't enjoy life, everything inside you will resist change, and the last thing you want is to actually make your life worse or miserable.

Exercise:

Think about who you like to take advice from, and why. Is this person already in the place where you want to be? Does this person perhaps exude a certain authority? What can you learn from them? Think about what you want to learn in the first place and then see if you can find someone to point you in the right direction.

Take care of yourself, lovely – you are so worth it!!! Until next week,

Mandy

There are as many ways to do things as there are people.

Letter 15

Hi lovely,

Today, I'd like to give you an idea of how my thought processes work.

In today's world, where the pace of life often demands that everything happens pretty fast if not yesterday, and phrases like 'speed dating' or 'high-speed internet' are part of our everyday vocabulary, it seems I may sometimes be the exception.

I love being able to think in peace and quiet. When and how I feel like it. Just think. Not because I plan to present a finished product or offer a solution at the end of this thinking process, but because I enjoy thinking for thinking's sake.

Nowadays, many people are actually afraid to take a good look at themselves, to question who they are, and to imagine alternative scenarios for themselves (I'm talking about positive scenarios here, as negative thinking is practically second nature to most people). Things that might happen if they only dared to change something, never mind actually enjoying what this (imagined) change might bring.

Have you ever heard of the book I'm off Then by Hape Kerkeling (translated from the German by Shelley Frisch)? In this book, the author describes his experience of undertaking the Camino de Santiago pilgrimage. I listened to the audio book that Hape himself narrated and it really got me thinking. Although I am a person of faith, would I want to go on a pilgrimage myself? I thought about it some more. Going on such a journey on my own would be unthinkable for me, being the little scared cat that I am. I mean, what about all those dangers lying in wait for a woman for one thing? Nope, not really a thought I relished. I could imagine going with my husband, but why on earth would he volunteer to do a pilgrimage of the Camino with me and walk hundreds of miles when we could quite happily go to Norway for a bit of hiking and fishing? Sure, he would do it for my sake, but that would be the only reason. And apart from anything else, I think it would be quite difficult to walk with him as we would probably walk at a different pace anyway.

But why would it have to be Spain? There are so many pilgrimage routes. And then I got to thinking – why go on an actual pilgrimage route at all when you can just as easily go for a walk through the woods around the corner from home? It may be on a smaller scale, but the intention could be the same.

In fact, I don't think it really matters where you go, but a lot of people seem to be unable to just go for a walk for the fun of it with no particular destination in mind. That's why a pilgrimage suits these people perfectly, at some point they will inevitably reach their destination. Speaking here from personal experience, I think (here we go again) that the actual physical goal is irrelevant, but the mental goal is paramount. When I go for a walk on my own, and I don't mean one with a planned itinerary, I'm forced to confront myself and reflect.

I've often found that this is what happens: I set off for the woods or the beach and, at first, everyday matters start swirling round my mind, thoughts like: What should we have for dinner? What do I still need to get? What else do I have to do? But the longer I walk, the more likely I am to allow other thoughts to enter my mind that go that little bit deeper below the surface: Am I happy? Why? Why not? What could or would I like to change? What do I want to achieve? What, if anything, do these things have in common? How are they connected? Then, I just let my mind wander, totally relaxed, and soon I experience a feeling of liberation from the trials and tribulations of modern life – the life in which I rarely have the time to think.

From time to time, I meet up with my good friend and business partner on a Monday morning to share our ideas over a cup of tea. We simply let our thoughts materialize, take shape and flow, vocalizing them as they come – and are quite often surprised by how inspired and motivated we feel at the end of our 'thinktank' session with all those new ideas buzzing round our heads. It's our opportunity to reenergize and gather fresh inspiration from within. We are all full of good ideas, but if we never take the time to discover them and hear them out, we automatically have to rely on other people and their ideas. And let's be honest, nobody has better ideas for our own lives than we do, because we know ourselves best.

Although it's sometimes hard to be by ourselves, and to have to deal with any problems there may be as well, the sooner we do face ourselves and these problems, the sooner they will be resolved. Procrastinating only allows things to keep weighing us down and yet our aim is to feel free.

Exercise:

This week, go for a walk on your own without having a particular destination in mind and allow your thoughts to flow, even the negative ones. Fully immerse yourself and enjoy the process – you may just be surprised at the ideas that come to you and the unexpected ways you find of resolving any problems.

Take care of yourself, lovely – you are so worth it!!! Until next week,

Mandy

Thinking – the talking of the soul with itself.

Plato

Letter 16

Hi lovely,

Over the past year, I've heard a lot of "if and when" sentences.

Here are just a few examples:

1. When I have children, I'm sure I'll be able to enjoy Christmas again.
2. When I've cleared out the house, I'll be able to breathe again.
3. When I finish my exams, I'll finally be able to focus on other things again.
4. If I lose XX pounds, I'll revive my sex life with my husband.
5. When the new year begins, I'll change everything.
6. If I were a millionaire, I'd be happy because I'd be able to fulfil my every wish and do as I please.

It often makes me sad when I read or hear these "if and when" sentences, because I always have the feeling that these people are putting their lives on hold. Then, I'm reminded of my first marriage and the kind of thoughts I had back then:

'When we get our second car and have redecorated our home, been on holiday and returned fully refreshed to make a new start, our marriage is bound to work again!'

And what happened? We bought the second car, we redecorated our flat, we went on holiday – and then we got divorced.

Being happy or not is very much about making a conscious choice. We may not be able to influence our external circumstances, but we can decide how we react to them.

For example, if my husband doesn't always treat me the way I'd like to be treated and I don't say anything, then it's my own fault if nothing changes.

If I want to lose weight but do nothing about it, I only have myself to blame for not making any changes to my lifestyle.

If I'm faced with a problem and I'm not willing to change the mindset that caused the problem in the first place, then that's my lookout if I don't find a solution.

A dear friend of mine has a really great catchphrase. When asked how she's doing, she always replies, 'I'm always fine, and if not, I change something!'

What I really want to say is that you are the one that determines EACH AND EVERY SECOND of your life. You decide how you want to live, what you want to do and don't want to do. You alone have your life in your hands. If you don't like something, change it. Don't wait for other people or circumstances to change. Keep your hands on the wheel so you can drive whichever way you like.

Let's take another look at those examples from the beginning:

1. When I have children, I'm sure I'll be able to enjoy Christmas again.

Why wait so long? Maybe you'll never end up having children. You say you want to enjoy Christmas? Then, just go ahead and do it! Why not invite your friends and family round for Christmas drinks. Put some soothing music on, maybe read each other a poem or two, enjoy reminiscing together. Decorate your home. Make yourself a hot chocolate in the evening when you get home from work and read a Christmas story or watch a Christmas movie. Take pleasure in giving someone a present. You'll soon see you don't need to wait for anything. Create a peaceful festive atmosphere of your own to enjoy now.

2. When I've cleared out the house, I'll be able to breathe again.

Why wait until it's done? Take a deep breath, in and out. You've already made your decision, and everything else will follow. Enjoy every centimeter you clear, but don't put yourself under pressure and don't wait until everything is done to feel good. That would be a waste of your precious time.

3. When I finish my exams, I'll finally be able to focus on other things again.

Whether there's an exam coming up or not, you won't be busy 24 hours a day. Set times to concentrate fully on your work and then reward yourself. If you know that you're going to the cinema with your friend in the evening, you'll probably find it easier to concentrate, because you know that it's only for a limited time and not forever. Life will keep happening around us, whether we have a particular thing that takes up a lot of time or not. The important thing is that we keep participating in life or otherwise it might just pass us by.

4. If I lose XX pounds, I'll revive my sex life with my husband.

Maybe your husband will lose all interest anyway if you keep putting him off. It's important that you love yourself just the way you are. Don't let a factor like your weight control your life. Talk to your husband, ask him for support – never underestimate the intimacy you get by talking about feelings.

5. When the new year begins, I'll change everything.

The best thing you can do is start right away, because EVERYTHING is rather a lot and you will need every second you can spare. Start small, get your priorities straight, and then get going. When the first cog, no matter how small, starts turning, everything else will start to move too. Celebrate every single success, because that's part of life. After all, it's all about the journey, not the destination.

6. If I were a millionaire, I'd be happy because I'd be able to fulfil my every wish and do as I please.

Are you sure you can't fulfil any of your wishes now? Do you really need a huge amount of money for each and every one?

I believe it's essential to really live life and enjoy it to the fullest in the here and now. We don't know when it will end. And if we keep putting things off, our lives will pass us by.

There will always be 'perfect' and 'impossible' moments in your life. You must learn to love them all, laugh at them and learn from them, because they are all part of life's rich tapestry. Learn to deal with them. Trying to ignore them usually only ends in even greater problems than those you had in the first place.

Exercise:

Think about what your own 'if and when' sentences are. Write each of them down and take a good look at them. Is there anything you can do by changing your way of thinking and behaving that will allow you to enjoy your life right now? Remember to find ways to make the journey fun too, it's the best way of making sure we stay motivated enough to reach our destination!

Take care of yourself, lovely – you are so worth it!!! Until next week,

Mandy

If you only walk on sunny days, you'll never reach your destination.

American saying

Letter 17

Hi lovely,

I've had an awful lot on my plate recently and I'd be lying if I said it hadn't been at all stressful. But to be honest, I believe there are two types of stress (well, in my life at least), and in my case it's definitely been the good kind.

Let's deal with the negative stress first and get it over and done with. I feel negative stress when I have to do things I don't enjoy much or I'm not at all good at – especially if there's a deadline involved. I can't just ignore these things because they are part of my life and normal everyday stuff, like getting on with my tax return or figuring out how to convert CDs to MP3 and then uploading them to my son's MP3 player.

So, what do I do in these situations? I look to see if can delegate these jobs – in this case, giving the tax return to the accountant to deal with. Yes, it costs money and if I knuckled down, I probably could manage it myself. But I really have no desire to do it whatsoever. I'd much rather go for a walk on the beach! However, if something can't be delegated it's always better to get on with it IMMEDIATELY. Why? Well, because if I keep putting something off, the task just strangely seems to get bigger and bigger and more difficult the longer I leave it.

I heard a great little story recently. It was about the metaphorical rucksack that we all carry around with us – every time we postpone something, we pop that something in our mental rucksack and carry on, but also carry on thinking about the things in the rucksack. Consequently, our load grows heavier and heavier and we find it difficult to move onto other tasks, because the old stuff starts weighing us down too much. But if we begin with a job we don't like and persevere until it's finally done, we'll be free to do all those other things, the more enjoyable things in life, while automatically reducing our levels of negative stress.

Now, what about positive stress? It's so important for us to test ourselves, push ourselves beyond our self-imposed limits and firmly out of our comfort zones in order to grow. After all, 'nothing ventured, nothing gained'. I'm sure you've heard that one before, right? I think there's a lot of wisdom in that saying.

When I think about how I used to sweat blood and tears when I had to cook for my family – deary me! And now you'll find me planning garden parties for more than a hundred people without even batting an eyelid.

My husband and I, for example, always like to host Christmas parties at our house from late November onwards. Obviously, this involves a lot of work (stress), but it's the kind of 'stress' we enjoy. It gives us such pleasure to see our guests really enjoy the food we've prepared as well as appreciating our festively decorated home or when they pause to read our Christmas cards for a moment, and reflect on the loving messages people have sent. There's no greater accolade. We also like to pat each other on the back afterwards, because we are both really happy and proud to be able to host such wonderful festive get-togethers. When we finally flop into bed exhausted, we always feel elated. Incidentally, we don't throw these parties just so we can stroke our egos afterwards, but because the people around us are important to us and this is our way of saying thank you to them for being part of our wonderful life. So, as you can see, that positive stress can definitely have additional benefits.

Exercise:

Just take a moment to think if you have a dream you've always wanted to fulfil, but the amount of work involved has put you off. Now let the scenario play out in your head. How would you feel if you did invest the time and effort and it worked out? Does it feel good? Then get to work!!! Remember - nothing ventured, nothing gained.

Take care of yourself, lovely – you are so worth it!!! Until next week,

Mandy

Letter 18

Hi lovely,

Yesterday, I felt a little overwhelmed. My head was spinning from all the work I had to do over the next few days – obviously, all of it to very tight deadlines.

So, cue the following monologue in my head:

'I'm going to have to let some people down, because it's just not going to work. There's no way I can get it all done – I simply don't have the time. But what choice do I have? Some things can't be put off and I gave my word. Okay, I need a piece of paper, a pen and a big cup of tea!'

So, while the water was boiling, I got my clipboard and paper and pen. I then made myself a cup of tea and started planning for the next few days. When is which deadline? What can I manage to do by then without any help? Who do I need to ask if I do need help? What is the absolute number one priority? And so it went on – for two hours!!! Needless to say, this also included all the usual everyday tasks, meal planning, childcare, festivities – which should always go ahead despite everything, because I'm not putting the things I enjoy in life on hold because of work.

Now, you might say: 'Really Mandy? You could have got something done in those two hours you spent writing your masterplan. What a waste of time.' To which I can only reply

'But no, coming up with a plan first helped me to focus and calm down.'

This has just reminded me of a quote I once saw on a postcard:

Everyone said: 'It can't be done!'

Then someone came along who didn't know and just did it anyway.

Now that I have a detailed plan, I can concentrate on what is important and what needs to be done on any given day. I can ignore everything else because I know that I have allocated a certain time frame for each task. This is smart from a psychological perspective, as I would otherwise be hopelessly overwhelmed.

Then my superpower (you remember: FOCUS) comes into play and I will achieve the impossible rather than just retreating into my cubbyhole. And the fact that after these days of hard slog a wonderful weekend with my husband awaits helps me to keep going. It's the light at the end of the tunnel, as it were. At the end of the day, I'll be able to pat myself on the back for having managed to get it all done, yet again, with a feeling of irrepressible pride and joy every time to boot.

Here is a small example of when it pays to prepare:

If I'm running out of something, I make sure to stock up on it again in good time. I fill up salt shakers again as soon as they're empty. Then, when I cook and speed is of the essence, I won't be thrown off track because I'll already have everything to hand. These things may seem trivial, but they are important if you want everything to run smoothly. So, this is the thing: it doesn't matter how small the cog is that we turn, it will always influence the result. So, let's make sure that we turn the cog in the right direction.

Exercise:

If you have a big challenge to tackle, invest a little time in preparation and planning. This will give you an overview of what you need to do, which in turn will reassure you and allow you to approach the task at hand feeling calmer and more relaxed.

Don't forget – make sure there is a reward waiting for you at the end of it all!!!

Take care of yourself, lovely – you are so worth it!!! Until next week,

Mandy

In preparing for battle, I have always found that plans are useless, but planning is indispensable.

Dwight D. Eisenhower

Letter 19

Hi lovely,

In my last letter, I was telling you how important I think it is to have a plan to help keep us grounded and to stop us from feeling overwhelmed or even doubting our own sanity because of the sheer hecticness of life around us.

I learned something very important a few years ago: just because I do everything by myself doesn't make me some kind of superhero. In fact, quite the opposite is true. I'm an idiot if I think I always have to do everything by myself, especially if I end up cracking under the strain.

I mean, what's the point if all I'm doing is falling into bed every night, utterly exhausted, with a headache already brewing as soon as I start thinking about the following day? That's not a fulfilled life, at least not the way I see things.

I've always worked a lot, but recently I've also been able to start enjoying my life properly without letting the thought of all the millions of jobs that seem to need doing spoil things. Let me give you an example:

We have a large garden which I've never really been able to see as a thing of beauty – in fact, it's always represented work, more work and then some stress thrown in for good measure. (I mean, what would other people think if they saw those weeds taking over?) Then there's also the fact that I suffer from hay fever. But last summer all that changed and

I ended up having so much fun with my family. We built ourselves a small pool, and took the time in the afternoon or evening to jump in before drying off in the sun on the patio. It was wonderful – even though those weeds were still there. Why did it suddenly not matter? How come I could appreciate the garden instead of despairing? It's very simple. I realized that I no longer had to play the superhero and take on the world single-handedly. I was doing stuff I didn't enjoy that left me feeling frustrated and fed up. And yet hadn't I promised myself that I was going to live life to the full and stop trying to make it as difficult for myself as humanly possible? So, I got some help. I asked my family to take over certain jobs like weeding, and watering the plants in the evenings.

Then, I told one of my classes that I wanted a gardener for Christmas that could give my garden a good going-over and change it to suit my needs. And voila! It worked out perfectly, it just so happened that two of the ladies on my course were in fact gardeners and thought it was a brilliant idea for a present. The other course participants then contributed some plants. Perfect! All of those grasses that I was highly allergic to were removed, and the beds were redesigned for low maintenance so that my family and I now have a lot less work to do.

But why had my life just improved that one little bit more? Because I opened my mouth! Because I made my needs known! Because I was worth taking more care of!

I'm already looking forward to all the fun we're going to have in our garden next year.

But it's not just about the garden, it's about my attitude towards things.

Let's take a look at a different example from my life:

It used to be that when I came home from work on Friday afternoons, I didn't exactly look forward to the great weekend that lay ahead. I often have a lot to do during the week and I'm not at home all the time to keep the house clean. Of course, everyone does their best and helps out, but to be honest: Nobody sees the dirt like I do. I'd often talked to my husband about having a cleaner to which his initial reaction was: 'Let's not waste the money. We can all pitch in.'

Fair enough. So, we tried out a cleaning rota. To cut a long story short, it didn't really work out the way I'd imagined it, and besides, it often caused arguments and tempers to fray.

And since I'm a woman who takes 100% responsibility for her life, I sat down with my husband and we discussed it again. Once we had gone through a detailed list of both of our commitments it was clear how little time was left in the week to take on the cleaning.

Often, it's not even about the cleaning itself, we usually manage somehow, despite family and work, if we put our minds to it. It's more about the mental energy taken by the task of cleaning and organizing a household.

I was striving for inner peace. I wanted to know and not hope that the place would be clean when I got home, and that I could just get on with my other priorities and enjoy some free time.

My dream was to get my youngest child out of day care on Friday afternoons, go to the library with him as usual and then have a coffee at a cafe afterwards. I fulfilled this part of my dream a long time ago, but the next part only recently. Before we go home, we stop at the florist and buy a small bouquet of flowers. And the only job I have left now, when I get home, is to put this bouquet in a vase on the table and enjoy the weekend.

Of course, money is a relevant issue here because this luxury comes at a price. However, once I'd worked out what a cleaner would cost me and how much free time and, above all, the quality of life I would gain by having one, I was convinced that it would prove to be a worthwhile investment for me.

Exercise:

Is there something in your life that you are very reluctant to do and that you could perhaps delegate to someone else? If nobody was there to judge you, what kind of tasks would you outsource? Maybe a babysitter for a couple of hours each day or a meal delivery service. Would outsourcing a task leave you more time to focus on your priorities? Invest in yourself! Take care of yourself, lovely – you are so worth it!!! Until next week,

Mandy

Letter 20

Hi lovely,

I really had to laugh out loud when I saw this on a calendar recently:

To quote SHAKESPEARE'S HAMLET act 4, scene 5, verse 28: "NO."

I'm in the process of learning to quote this off by heart so that I can courteously (and with a chuckle) turn something down when someone asks me to do something.

Our time is such a precious commodity and yet on the rare occasion when we do have some spare, we tend to spend it on doing this, that and the other for everyone else and not using it for our own benefit or interests.

Even though we women have a lot on our plate these days and a great deal is demanded of us, we still have a lot more resources than our grandmothers and great-grandmothers ever had. Yes, yes, I know: life was different back then, most people stayed at home, etc., but let me have a little fun with this game!

Below are some of the things we have at our disposal nowadays (to name but a few examples):

1. Childcare from birth to preschool to after-school clubs
2. Washing machines
3. Tumble dryers
4. Dishwashers

5. Internet
6. Cheap flights
7. Money to pay for services that help us

And what do we do with all these luxuries? We simply saddle ourselves with more work instead of using the time we could otherwise spend on ourselves.

Hand on heart, who reads a book while the dishwasher is on or goes for a walk while the washing machine is doing a load? No one? That's what I thought. Oh, hang on, you do? Well, good for you! Think we could all take a leaf out of your book in that case …

Every time someone asks if I can do them a favor I often say yes, even if I don't feel like it at all! Why do I do that?? I can't say that I don't have any time, because it's written all over my face when I lie. But it would be so rude to just say, 'No, I've something better to do.'

Now that I've decided to follow your lead, you must tell me what you do about the guilty conscience part. No way! That's your secret? Oh, I think I may just have heard that line somewhere before – in an advert:

Because I'm worth it!

Right, so now I know your secret and have that fantastic quote in my head, I can forge ahead knowing that my time will remain MY time in future.

Exercise:

Are there times when you find it difficult to say no? Do you sometimes feel bad or guilty? When in doubt about taking the little precious time you have for yourself, just remember the slogan from the advert 'because I'm worth it!' With that in mind, banish that guilty conscience or any negative thoughts and just say NO, if and when it's right for you!

Take care of yourself, lovely – you are so worth it!!! Until next week,

Mandy

The ability to say no is the first step towards freedom

Nicolas Chamfort

Letter 21

Hi lovely,

Thanks again for reminding me of this last week – a slogan we can each apply and practice saying:

Because I'm worth it!

What a marvelous motto to live by! As a matter of fact, I actually managed to use the time once when the dishwasher, the washing machine and the dryer were running (that's what I call efficient) to do absolutely nothing.

Yes, I know, I could have used the time to do some exercise, go for a walk or read, but I honestly didn't feel like doing anything at all.

I just sat on the sofa in the sun and looked out of the window. It was very quiet in the house (obviously the door to the utility room was closed) and as I sat there my thoughts started to wander.

It felt great to listen and not hear anything. It was so good to know that I didn't have to do anything at all. The warmth of the sun streaming through the window was so relaxing. I didn't care that the window wasn't exactly clean and that I was doing nothing constructive. In fact, that was the point. It was fascinating to be able to focus on my body and mind in peace and quiet.

In fact, without meaning to, I think I was meditating, don't you?

And then, in this state of calm and balance, I started daydreaming.

I imagined what the coming weeks and months would be like. All those great things I was going to do and experience. And I was filled with a great sense of joy and happiness.

Well, you can probably guess what happened next: without even the slightest sense of guilt, I fell asleep on the sofa, basking in the warmth of the sun. And when I woke up about twenty minutes later, I felt free, balanced, happy, inspired and full of energy.

I was also consumed by a wave of gratitude. I was so very grateful that by reminding you to focus on yourself, you had reminded me to focus on ME and not always on everyone else. I felt grateful for the way I live and for all those people in my life who enrich it – my husband and my children, my parents and grandparents, everyone who has been part of my life all these years, making me the person I am today and, above all, the person I love: ME!

I am a great person, just like YOU. We are given so many gifts in life and often we don't even notice them because we are so busy being busy.

Life is great!!

Exercise:

Simply take time out from the life around you for some quality YOU time. Do absolutely nothing and enjoy (re)connecting with the wonderful person that is you.

Take care of yourself, lovely – you are so worth it!!! Until next week,

Mandy

Peace draws life in, unrest drives it away.

Gottfried Keller

Letter 22

Hi lovely,

Yesterday evening, something rare happened in that all five of us actually managed to gather together on the sofa for some family viewing, which, on this occasion, was a cooking show with the chef Jamie Oliver. This family time made me really happy, especially as our oldest child has already left home and just happened to be visiting. I was on the right, with the youngest on my left, followed by our oldest, then the middle one and at the other end, my husband. A quite harmonious picture from where I was sitting. But if someone else had been looking on they may have seen something quite different – i.e. the time. It was already very late and our little one is only four. He couldn't sleep so he'd come back down again to snuggle up under my blanket. And it was lovely.

I know people whose children sleep at 7 p.m. sharp, no messing around. That's very impressive. I always get tips from all kinds of people telling me how I can do things better – that's just great, especially when these people don't even have any kids of their own!!!

Anyway, I thought to myself: 'Nope, this is right for us and for this moment in time. I mean, what's the worst thing that can happen? So, maybe the little one won't be able to get out of bed in the morning and I won't be able to take him to day care. Well, that's not the end of the world. He'll just have to have a day off and I'll rearrange things to fit around that.'

And I wouldn't have had this one moment with everyone sitting together and enjoying each other's company if I'd wanted to be like other people or if I'd wanted to assert my authority as a mother ('But you have to go to bed when I say so!'). There is a time for everything and this moment was there to be enjoyed.

I learned a long time ago that comparing myself with others only makes me unhappy.

The fact is: every person is different, has different life circumstances, sets different priorities, thinks and acts differently, has different hopes and desires. Who decides whether one person is doing it right and the other one wrong? When I was a new mother, I was apparently a prime target for unwanted advice. Everyone, seriously EVERYONE, knew better and seemed to do things differently. They couldn't help themselves from painting the scenes of absolute horror that were bound to be the consequence if I didn't let my child scream and cry, make it sleep in its own bed in its own room immediately, never mind the unimaginable of giving it sugar and all that other stuff.

Seriously? This is MY or rather OUR life we're talking about here. The only really good advice I ever got was: 'You and your husband have to agree. What everybody else thinks and does doesn't matter.'

Indeed, in our house, bedtime can often be quite late, especially in summer when life is primarily outdoors and it stays light for so long.

In the past, I genuinely used to worry, because I thought I might somehow be 'harming' the kids if they weren't in bed by 7 pm at the latest and if I chose to give them an ice cream instead of an apple.

But hey ho, luckily, I seem to be getting wiser and definitely more relaxed as the years go by. We have such a good life and we're able to adapt to the various situations it throws at us. So, if it does happen to be getting on a bit, so what? Worse things happen at sea. And if the kids live entirely on chocolate at Christmas, chances are they'll survive that too.

Our pediatrician once told me I had nothing to worry about. There are children who need 14 hours of sleep and there are children who make do with nine hours or even less. It was up to me to decide if having a "wakeful" child was a blessing or a curse.

Like everything else in life, it is our choice how we react to things, and I've decided that it's a blessing. Obviously, the idea of a lie-in in at the weekend is a distant one – but on the other hand, it just means we have more time together as a family if the little one wakes up nice and early. And if I want to feel rested, I just have to go to bed earlier. Again, it's my decision and I have to take the consequences of my actions.

Exercise:

Take some time and examine why you do certain things that don't resonate with you or why you don't do other things you would love to do. Is it because somebody has said something that has made you feel bad in the past? Please remember, lovely, that this is your life and your life only. You are the one person you will spend the rest of your life with. People come and go, don't let them make your decisions for you. What brings YOU joy? What do YOU want to BE, DO and HAVE? Make a list!

Take care of yourself, lovely – you are so worth it!!! Until next week,

Mandy

Everyone should become blessed in their own way.

Frederick the Great

Letter 23

Hi lovely,

I'm really excited. We've already started our annual planning for the year ahead. I know it's still a long way off, but we always have so much fun doing it, and today was the perfect day to start.

Have I ever told you how we go about it? Well, I place a big sheet of A3 paper in the middle of the kitchen table, a small bucket of colored pencils beside it, and off we go. Everyone is allowed to write down or draw what they would like to do next year.

So, this is what we came up with:

Amongst other things, our youngest one's wishes included seeing his godmother, going on a trip to London, and visiting our friends' farm.

My husband wanted to go to the Wacken Open Air Festival, Norway to go fishing, do a bike trip along the Kiel Canal and go on a family camping holiday with all of us.

Some of the things I wished for were a two-week family holiday in England, a family trip to Milan, a big tea party in the garden and an Easter brunch.

A lot of our wishes naturally overlapped.

By the end of it, the sheet of paper was completely full, and we'd had so much fun doing it! But a wish list alone won't get us very far, so the next step was the calendar.

Everything we could give a date to or a certain time period was entered in the calendar. We then set our priorities.

Now, you might think that this is a lot of travelling and ask yourself how we intend to finance it. Well, I can tell you this: with forward planning and lots of friends!

When we travel somewhere, we often only have to pay for the flights or the train tickets and then stay overnight with friends. And vice versa, of course. When friends come to us, they only have to pay for the journey. We pick them up from the airport or train station, give them a place to stay, enjoy meals together, and if they want to go on excursions, we lend them our car. It's all about give and take. And because my husband and I have invested many, many years in our friendships and relationships, we can now enjoy the rewards that come with them.

At the start of a new year, a lot of people make a list of their New Year resolutions or intentions, which I've noticed generally involve giving up something, for example, cigarettes, alcohol, fast food, etc.

We do things differently. We plan our AMAZING LIFE and even if we don't manage everything in one year, we do it the following year or the year after. But in the meantime, we can already start planning and saving up. And let's be honest, anticipation is often one of the most enjoyable parts of the process.

Exercise:

It's time to enjoy that wonderful feeling of anticipation by planning your own AMAZING LIFE now. So, grab a piece of paper, some pens and go for it, no holds barred. Remember, once you have your list of wishes, schedule them into your diary and then think about the resources you have available to you to turn your dreams into achievable goals.

Take care of yourself, lovely – you are so worth it!!! Until next week,

Mandy

A dream that is given a date becomes a goal.

A goal that is divided into small steps becomes a plan.

And a plan followed by an action becomes a reality.

Letter 24

Hi lovely,

I'm still feeling a bit shocked. I was sitting on the bus on Monday morning on the way to the train station, thinking about a lovely meetup I'd had on the Sunday. The man opposite me asks the woman next to him, 'What did you get up to this weekend?' to which she replies with a dismissive flick of her hand, 'Oh, nothing special. We went to the sauna on Friday, the cinema on Saturday, and for an Italian meal with friends on Sunday.'

'Right, so, that's "nothing special,"' I thought. What exactly is special? A short trip to New York for shopping, in your own private jet???

And boom, I was right back in the prejudice trap. My first thought was: 'What the actual? You have no idea how good you have it!'

But the question is, was she just trying to impress the man next to her? I really don't know. I've been riding the same bus with this woman for months, and she is definitely someone you notice. She's always immaculately dressed and very stylish, often wearing perfectly coordinated outfits. Her hair looks amazing and her make-up is flawless, BUT she never smiles. She always looks bored – and now this remark. Who knows, maybe this woman works all hours, does tons of overtime, and going to the sauna, cinema and restaurants really is nothing to write home about from her point of view – but I can tell you, I was still shocked, nonetheless. Especially as I'd recently given a professional development course to a group of people reliant on the welfare system and who really have to watch every single penny. I think I was just totally stunned by the gaping chasm that had just opened up.

For the participants on my course, an ice cream was sometimes the highlight of the week and this woman on the bus seemed to have it all and didn't even appreciate it.

One more thing comes to mind: Do you remember the woman I was telling you about that we met at the birthday party the other day? The woman who was really wealthy? The one with the big house and the husband who made a shed load of money which allowed her to do whatever she fancied – and all she did was bitch and moan? The house was too big, the husband was away too often, the garden was too much work despite the gardener … And if you recall, she and her husband were trying to find a holiday destination and they couldn't agree on one because she found fault with everything, literally everything. It was just perverse. There's a person who has everything that money can buy and still isn't happy.

On the other hand, there are people who are so content with so little, as if they were living like royalty, as if they lacked for nothing – and at the same time, they radiate such an inner peace and kindness that it blows my mind.

Anyway, what happened on the bus and at that party prompted me to stop and take stock of my own life for once. I sat down and consciously thought about everything I have and actually own. Then I imagined what would happen if I lost all my possessions in a fire. And you know what? It wouldn't be the end of the world. Many things can easily be replaced and the memories of certain things would abide. For example, the memory of my grandmother's beautiful rose china, which I purposely use as often as possible to add the perfect finishing touch to tea parties. These memories are deeply rooted within me.

So, while I was sitting there and thinking about the "loss", a few quotes came to mind that you've almost certainly heard before, too.

1. You can't take it with you [or 'the last shirt has no pockets' as the Germans say].
2. The box won't be big enough to take it all with you.
3. You'll never see a U-Haul [removal van] behind a hearse.

The last quote is from Denzel Washington. He used that line in a graduation address at an American university.

And it's so true! The pharaohs may have been buried with everything they owned, but when we go, we'll only be wearing the clothes that others choose to dress us in.

When I think about it, all our possessions are only there to give us joy in this world.

Let me just repeat that: 'Our possessions are only meant to bring us joy NOW!'

There are two truths in that sentence that will change your life if you take them to heart.

· If you own things that bring you no joy but burden you, let them go. The only purpose of possessions in life is to give you joy.

· You will only be left with the things that are in your heart: memories and love.

So, I've decided that I am going to invest much more time and energy in my relationships, because I don't want to be without the people in my life who support me, care for me and, yes, who love me and whom I also love with all my heart. Furthermore, I'm not going to allow any object to burden me during my precious time here on earth.

I love you!

Exercise:
Take the time to sit down and really take stock of your life. Write a list of all the things you are grateful for and focus on the following: If you woke up tomorrow with only those things you had thanked the universe for, what would you want to make sure was included in that list?
Take care of yourself, lovely – you are so worth it!!! Until next week,

Mandy

People were created to be loved.
Things were created to be used.
The reason why the world is in chaos
is because things are being loved,
and people are being used.

Dalai Lama

Letter 25

Hi lovely,

Have you ever watched the Darren Daily videos by Darren Hardy? Do you know what really left an impression on me from one of these? This sentence:

No matter what your past looks like,

your future is like a blank canvas.

When I think about how often I've messed up in my life and how many wrong decisions I've made, I know they've all served to make me the woman I am today, one I'm also very proud of. I find the above quote so infinitely reassuring. Even if yesterday was pretty rubbish, tomorrow can still be great.

Funnily enough, I often have this feeling shortly after Christmas having eaten my way through a mountain of delicious food, which unfortunately includes way too many unhealthy items. Not to mention all those yummy sweets that seem to be just about everywhere, lying in wait to tempt me. But it's not that bad; just because I couldn't resist temptation at Christmas doesn't mean I'll find myself being shoved back in the sea by Greenpeace come summer, mistaking me for a stranded whale. Yeah, it's alright for you to laugh!

No, seriously, it's nice to know that every day brings with it new, exciting opportunities.

On a personal level, I really appreciate the fact that I've learned to change my behavior any time I want, if I choose to. After all, a lot of people wait for the New Year to make their resolutions to change – e.g. start eating healthier food, exercise more or settle a dispute and make up with someone. However, the best time to restore balance to our lives or to set out on the path to a better YOU is NOW. Just go for it and if it goes wrong, just start again tomorrow and try again and again and again until it works out.

Jim Rohn, the American motivational speaker, once asked his audience how long a baby tries to learn to walk before it gives up. The audience laughed because a baby obviously tries for as long as it takes to learn to walk. When I think about it, we've already achieved so much in our lives: we've learned to walk, to speak, to love, etc. So why do we sometimes think that something is too hard and we don't even bother trying?

Any exchange student who goes to a country whose language they don't speak will be very frustrated at the beginning of their exchange year. Maybe they won't understand much or even be able to communicate with anyone. But when the year is over, not only will they have learned the language of that country, but they will have had the opportunity to immerse themselves in a completely different culture and experience things they could never have imagined before. A year may sound like a long time at the beginning, but think how long it would normally take to become fluent in a language if we tried evening courses or online language courses. One year is nothing! Apart from that, that exchange year will boost an exchange student's self-confidence enormously.

In the past, I'd just about faint at the thought of having to sing in front of the whole school. Once in a while, I'd have a solo part in the choir. All I could hear would be the sound of blood rushing through my veins and my heart pounding. And nowadays? I can stand in front of thousands of people and say what I have to say. Did it take a long time to get over the fear of public speaking? Yes, it certainly did. Did I often have to start all over again? Of course, I did. But in the end, it was all worth it. I learned that people are basically quite well-meaning creatures. But if anyone is ever horrible to me, I know it's often because of their own insecurities. I've continued to grow and I'm really happy that I kept grabbing for the proverbial new canvas until my next painting met my expectations.

Besides, there are many people in the spotlight who have experienced their own trials and tribulations, i.e. tried over and over again...

After 1,000 unsuccessful attempts to develop a marketable light bulb, Edison allegedly remarked: 'I have not failed one thousand times. I have successfully discovered a thousand ways to NOT make a light bulb.'

Now, that's what I call perseverance.

Exercise:

If something doesn't work the first time or the first hundred times, don't give up. Just grab a new canvas and try again. Take care of yourself, lovely – you are so worth it!!! Until next week,

Mandy

I will either find a way, or make one!

Hannnibal

Letter 26

Hi lovely,

I'm an absolute sucker for inspiring quotes. And because I'm having so much fun accompanying you on your epic journey to your BEST SELF, I've decided to focus on one saying on each of the following topics over the next eight weeks:

1. Beginnings
2. Motivation
3. Perseverance
4. Success
5. Dreams
6. Goals
7. Self-awareness
8. Experience

Obviously, I'll be adding my two pennies' worth as the letters would otherwise be a little on the short side ;-)

Here is the quote to think about for BEGINNINGS:

It's not important how big the first step is, but the direction it takes.

(Author unknown)

Well, that's what I've always said! Even with baby steps we can reach our goal, but we have to take them and, above all, we have to know where we want to go!

In my workshops, I always use the following illustration.

As you know, I'm from Germany, where things are very much standardized. This actually helps me a lot when I'm doing my presentations.

Imagine you are standing at the bottom of a very long spiral staircase and looking up. At the top is your goal. It seems so incredibly far away that most people's initial reaction is one bordering on panic. However, as it often turns out, taking the first step is actually quite easy: for example, getting a travel catalogue to look for that dream holiday, perusing vacancies to find that job you always wanted. And thanks to those standardized steps, the first one is just as high as the second, fiftieth, hundredth and thousandth. This means that the effort we put into climbing the first step is exactly the same effort we have to put into climbing the forty-eighth step. And since we've already climbed the first step, we know that this is not an insurmountable hurdle.

Isn't that great? I think it's amazing!

- Set your goal
- Take the first step
- Carry on, one step at a time
- Reach your goal
- Done!

Yes, of course there are always a few workshop participants who insist: 'Yes, all well and good, but ...' But what? Oh, that kind of attitude really drives me nuts. Seriously!

Why all the "buts"? Why not just go ahead and take your chances, see if it works?

'That sounds too easy to be true.' That's something I hear a lot. But shall I let you into a little secret? It's actually quite easy once we adjust our mindset to focus on the task at hand, our goal. Once we've made up our minds and our hearts are set on reaching the goal, and we get stuck in and start chasing it, the rest often just follows suit. Life doesn't always have to be difficult – in fact, it's quite simple if we allow it to be.

A dear Italian friend gave me a blank notebook for my birthday. On the first page she had written the following:

Es geht bergauf:

Wenn etwas besser läuft, geht es bei den Deutschen bergauf. Ihr wollt es immer möglichst schwierig.

Bei uns Italienern geht es bergab. Ist doch viel einfacher.

Tonia Mastobuoni, Italy ☺

Literally translated:

It's going uphill:

When things are improving, Germans think of it as going "uphill".

You [Germans] always want everything to be as difficult as possible.

With us Italians, we think of it as "downhill" – that's so much easier!

Tonia Mastobuoni, Italy

There you go: It's all about attitude!

<u>Exercise</u>:

Ask yourself this question: Am I going in the right direction? Or do I need to change course to avoid missing my destination?

Take care of yourself, lovely – you are so worth it!!! Until next week,

Mandy

It's not important how big the first step is, but the direction it takes.

Letter 27

Hi lovely,

The next inspiring quote is about MOTIVATION:

You yourself are your own obstacle, rise above yourself!

(Hafez)

The following story on the subject of motivation is based on one from the book The Compound Effect by Darren Hardy. I like to use a slightly different version of this story in my workshops, because it illustrates so well what motivation actually means.

I lay a thirty-centimeter-wide plank on the floor in front of a participant and say, 'If you walk across the plank, I'll give you ten euros.'

She does it without giving it a second thought. After all, it's easy money.

Next, I lay the plank across two chairs to make a bridge, and raise my offer to twenty euros. The price is higher this time, because the plank is now off the floor, introducing a certain risk of falling.

She quickly assesses the height of the chairs and the risk of accidents, but this is such easy money that she crosses the plank.

Then I say to her, 'OK, now imagine that the plank spans the gap between two tower blocks. I'll raise my offer to two hundred euros. Would you cross it?'

She replies, 'No, the risk of falling is too great.'

I increase the price to two thousand euros, then two hundred thousand and finally to one million euros.

When I reach one million, she interjects with, 'Your offer is really tempting, but I'd be so afraid of losing my life.'

Then I set the following scene: 'You're standing on the roof of one tower block, your children are on the other. The tower block that your children are on is on fire. You can only save them by going across this plank. What would you do?'

The participant says without a moment's hesitation, 'I'd run across the plank and save my kids!'

The challenge and the risk involved have not changed, but the participant's reaction has. To save her children, she would risk everything. The money is not enough of an incentive for her to risk her life, but her children are.

When we commit to a goal, no matter how big it is, we can achieve it with the right motivation. And given the necessary incentive, nothing is impossible.

Talking of impossible, if you look it up in the dictionary, you will find that one of its many synonyms is "inconceivable" and this is the reason why, in my opinion, the word "impossible" should be deleted from the dictionary. Everything in life is conceivable. Everything we see around us has been imagined by someone at some point. Every invention, no matter how great or small, began with a thought!

Exercise:

Eradicate the word "impossible" from your vocabulary and allow yourself to feel inspired and motivated. Every time you catch yourself thinking this is impossible, remember that throughout history people have said that over and over again until somebody has shown up and proved them wrong – flying, walking on the moon, a computer in your pocket, etc. Don't think why me? Think why NOT me?! Everything is possible if you believe it is!

Take care of yourself, lovely – you are so worth it!!! Until next week,

Mandy

You yourself are your own obstacle, rise above yourself!

Hafez

Letter 28

Hi lovely,

The next inspiring quote addresses the topic of PERSEVERANCE:

Nothing great is ever achieved without much enduring. (Catherine of Siena)

The quote below is much in the same vein as the above:

If you don't feel like starting over again, then don't give up.

(Author unknown)

How often have I been annoyed with myself for starting something and then failing to see it through? For example, starting pelvic floor training – I approach it with good intentions and the 'this time it will definitely work out' mantra only to find that after a few weeks, I'm too tired by the evening to actually do my exercises and end up leaving it for the day after and then the day after that. And suddenly, three months have passed, the hay fever season starts and I find myself having to squeeze my legs together very tightly indeed when I sneeze to avoid having an accident. And then I find myself thinking: 'Why? Why on earth didn't I just stick to it???'

I know, I know, those ifs, buts and maybes …

The simple fact is that if you start something but don't finish it, it's unlikely to give you the result you hoped for.

I was taught that if I'm going to do or start something, I should always do it properly. I pride myself on the fact that people can rely on me and the way I work. I would never dream of delivering something half-finished.

But I'm only human after all, and those pelvic floor exercises, or any other form of exercise for that matter, sometimes seem to be conspiring against me. So, what do I do about it? Well, I just start over from scratch (think back to the blank canvas). And I'll keep starting over and over again until I've finally done what I set out to do. I'm sure that at the end of it all, there will be a big reward waiting for me with my name on it! Then I'll look back and realize that actually, it wasn't that difficult after all. I really shouldn't have thrown in the towel time and time again.

After all, if I have to start from scratch every single time that means investing an awful lot of energy at the outset to get a project up and running properly.

Let's compare this to a rocket launch. At the beginning, an inordinate amount of energy has to be used to even get the rocket off the ground. But after a little perseverance, the rocket builds up momentum and only needs comparatively little energy to keep flying. Unfortunately, in my case though, I often give up shortly before reaching the momentum stage and then have to expend a lot of energy once again to relaunch. In other words, it would be much easier to just hang in there!!!

So, with that in mind, I wish you all the staying power you need for all of your projects so that the momentum carries you wherever you want to go.

<u>Exercise</u>:

The next time you start something, and you feel the urge to give up, hold out a little longer. Once you get going, your own momentum will want to carry you forwards and will. So, keep going – you've got this!

Take care of yourself, lovely – you are so worth it!!! Until next week,

Mandy

Nothing great is ever achieved without much enduring.

Catherine of Siena

Letter 29

Hi lovely,

The next inspiring quote relates to the subject of SUCCESS:

Action is the universal language of success.

(Steve Maraboli)

There's really not a lot more to add to this. If you want to succeed, you have to do something about it, you can't just sit around waiting for something to happen of its own accord. It's up to you to take the initiative and start taking control of your life.

All the great books I've read, the audio books I've listened to and seminars and workshops I've attended would be an absolute waste of time if I didn't put everything I've learned from all of these sources into practice.

I lead a wonderful life because I've worked hard for it. And I know you can do this too – and will! After all, you read these letters, among other things, because you want to create the life of your dreams, because you are eager to know more and learn from others. Learning is a life-long pursuit, but nothing will change if you don't take action!

Exercise:

Just do it!

Take care of yourself, lovely – you are so worth it!!! Until next week,

Mandy

Action is the universal language of success.

Steve Maraboli

Letter 30

Hi lovely,

DREAMS are the subject of the next inspiring quote:

It's never too late to be what you might have been.

(George Eliot)

Although the word "dream" isn't actually used in this quote, it's still about dreams and taking action. As touched on last week, a wish or dream alone is not enough to make it happen. You have to act as well. This quote takes the idea one step further, effectively giving us permission to make our dreams come true at any time, no matter how young or old we are.

The internet is full of inspiring stories about people who pursued their dreams late in life, turning their passions into reality – like becoming a student at the tender age of 90 plus and writing a doctoral thesis, or becoming an author who publishes their first work at 94. It really doesn't matter how old we are or why we do something or haven't done something before. The main thing is that we just do it when the opportunity arises.

Not so long ago, we were talking at home about how stupid (narrow-minded) we thought it was that a carpet salesman we had recently encountered had said, 'Why would you want to buy a new carpet for a 96-year-old? That's pointless.' Why would someone even say that, more like? Even if that

96-year-old can only enjoy it for one more day, who cares? On that day, that person is happy.

The idea of surrounding myself every day for the rest of my life with people and things I love fills me with joy. I'm so very humbled and proud of every single person who dares to pursue their dreams and make them reality. As we know, nothing in life is impossible if you put your mind to it. Although we may sometimes find ourselves facing challenging situations, it's always our decision as to how we react to them.

Some people really do have to wait until they are over 90 to go to university, perhaps because their late partners hadn't allowed it. Isn't it wonderful that these people didn't just stick their heads in the sand and say: 'Oh, it's too late now. It's not worth it anymore.' I admire and know many people who have had obstacles put in their way in life and who, despite everything, have never lost sight of their dreams and made them come true at the first opportunity.

Exercise:

What have you always dreamt about doing? How can you set the wheels in motion and start making them reality?

Take care of yourself, lovely – you are so worth it!!! Until next week,

Mandy

It's never too late to be what you might have been.

George Eliot

Letter 31

Hi lovely,

Today's inspiring quote is about GOALS:

If you always do what you can already do, you'll always remain who you already are.

(Author unknown)

I know a slightly different version of this quote, which has a similar sentiment: 'If you always do what you've always done, you'll always get what you've always got.' (That automatically makes me think of the film Titanic. No matter how often I watch that film, the captain always runs into the same iceberg; he just doesn't seem to learn ☺)

Albert Einstein was supposed to have once said that the definition of insanity is doing the same thing over and over again and expecting different results.

Doing the same thing again and again and expecting a different outcome each time sounds quite logical at first, but in practice it's actually quite difficult. Or at least that's how it seems to me. I sometimes catch myself making the same mistake over and over again and still wonder why I end up with the same rubbish outcome. (This certainly used to be true in some of my relationships!)

However, if I take the time to analyze and make myself aware of what I'm actually doing and what the consequences of my actions will be, I have a chance of changing my behavior to achieve a different result.

I'm just thinking about whether an example comes to mind… Yes, here's one! Almost every day I try to be more relaxed and to create harmony by giving other people the opportunity to do things the way they want to do them. But this means they don't do it the way I would like them to, so I 'correct' them, because my way (at least in my imagination) is the only proper way to do things. Now that I'm seeing that in black and white, I realize how very arrogant that sounds. But then my second thought is: 'But it's also true though in some respects – I know more about XYZ, because I have more experience and my way of working always produces excellent results.' This brings me to the following conclusion: I do things myself but get stressed out because of the extra work. The others feel patronized and inadequate. The general mood is pretty bad.

In order to achieve my goal of "serenity and harmony", I'm forced to change my way of thinking.

So, let me try again from the beginning.

I set a goal. I let the relevant people find ways to achieve the goal themselves. I practice serenity and generosity of spirit. I allow room for mistakes so that others can also grow from their experiences. I feel good because I've fulfilled my role properly as head or leader (of the family, the company, the association, etc.). The others feel appreciated and empowered in who they are as people because I have shown my faith in them. Harmony is established. When I look at the tasks that need doing, they're not exactly rocket science. So, I can relax. There are no mistakes that can't be ironed out one way or another. It's not the end of the world if the work isn't done entirely perfectly. Ultimately, I have achieved my goal by changing my way of thinking.

I'm so grateful that I can share my thoughts with you and learn so much myself in the process.

The author Richard Bach once said that 'we teach best what we most need to learn.'

Exercise:

Think about if there is a lesson in something that is bothering you. Could you change the situation by looking at it from another angle? Could you change your way of thinking? Is there a lesson to be learned –to be grateful for?

Take care of yourself, lovely – you are so worth it!!! Until next week,

Mandy

If you always do what you can already do, you'll always remain who you already are.

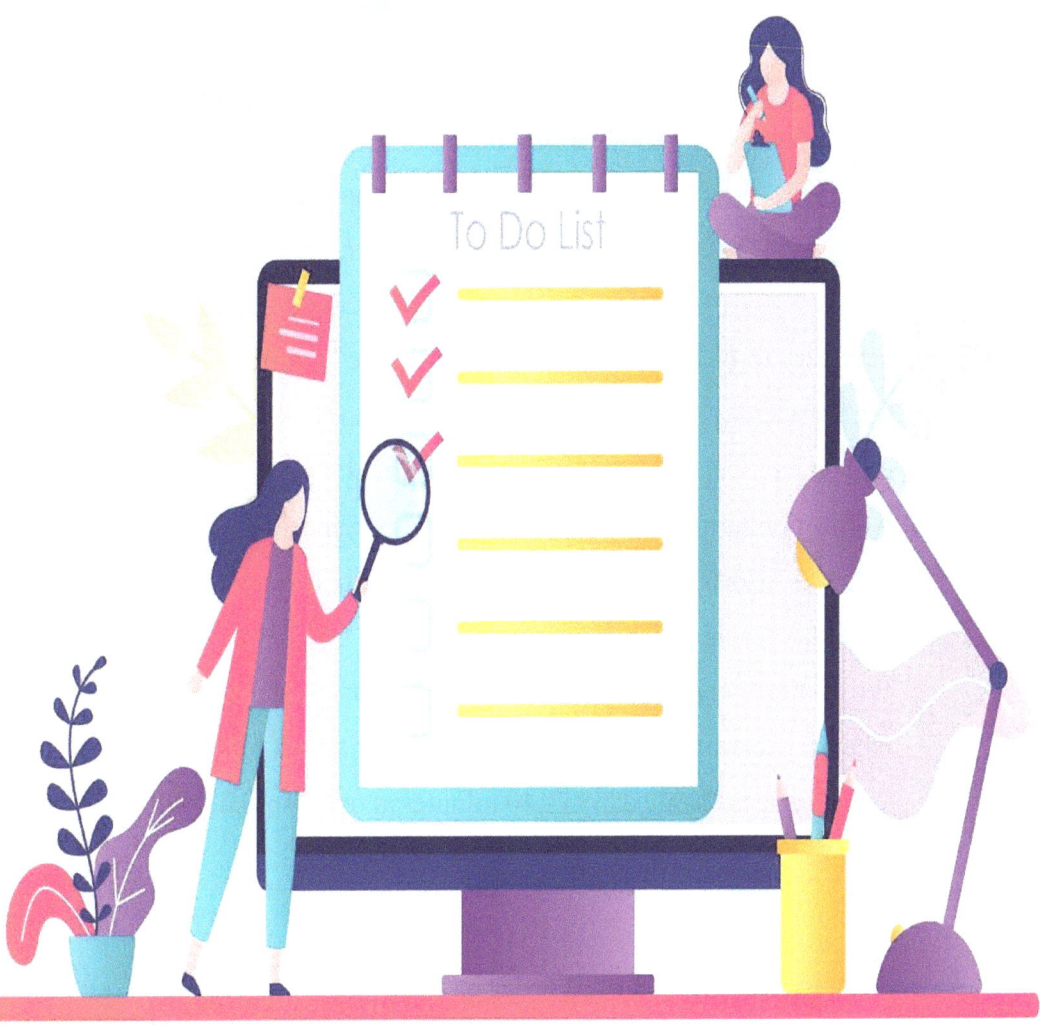

Letter 32

Hi lovely,

The inspiring quote I'd like to share with you this week is about SELF-AWARENESS:

It is not that we have so little time but that we lose so much… The life we receive is not short but we make it so.

(Lucius Annaeus Seneca)

I have to admit that I found it really difficult to decide which quote to use this week. Here are a few I had to choose from:

The only person you compete with is the one you see in the mirror! (Author unknown)

Sometimes you win and sometimes you learn! (Author unknown)

You cannot overtake anyone if you follow in their footsteps. (Francois Truffaut)

Don't try to be better than others. Try to be better than you were yesterday. (Author unknown)

As you can see, there are so many wonderful sayings that are worth pondering. The reason I chose Seneca's words, however, is that I just happen to be listening to an audio book about his teachings at the moment.

We all know that there are 24 hours in a day. Regardless of whether we are a doctor, an artist, a housewife or a ballerina, we all have the same daily 1440 minutes at our disposal. And yet we all make use of those minutes differently – and sometimes we don't make the most of them at all.

Who we are and what we have often have nothing to do with what we do but rather with what we don't do.

In one of my previous letters to you, I talked about how some people spend a lot of time in front of the television or computer screen, not getting enough exercise and, therefore, not achieving their goal of keeping fit and healthy. In that particular example, these people had two hours at their disposal: they chose to watch TV instead of doing some form of exercise.

I think you get my drift. We do have the time to do things. Once again, it's a matter of setting priorities when we have a goal in mind that we would like to achieve.

But let me reiterate that this is about us – you and me - and not about other people. We don't have to be like others. We are great just the way we are, whether or not we follow the current trends or fashion. We are who we are, and that's the way it should be.

However, if we really do want to change because we don't feel entirely satisfied or content with ourselves or our lives, then we can look at how others do it and ask ourselves if we can learn something from them.

Maths was never my forte, but I do understand the following equation:

Belief + action = miracle

Exercise:

Take a good look in the mirror: Do you love what you see in the reflection? The answer should be a resounding YES! If it isn't, take action now and make those changes to help you lead a more fulfilled life with a deeper sense of satisfaction. Take care of yourself, lovely – you are so worth it!!! Until next week,

Mandy

Letter 33

Hi lovely,

This is the last inspiring quote of our mini-series and refers to the subject of EXPERIENCE.

You can chalk it up to experience.

(Arno Gummerlich)

Short but sweet, this one is actually from my dad and it is what he tends to say more than once when I've had what I consider to be a bad experience – for example, when I think a job interview hasn't gone that well or I've bought the wrong thing after all; but equally it applies to mishaps or accidents, bad relationships, events that haven't quite turned out the way I thought they would.

I mentioned near the beginning of these letters that I was an exchange student (many moons ago). Before I did my year abroad, I attended a meeting designed to help me and my fellow exchange students prepare for what lay ahead. This included being warned about the negative aspects of doing an exchange, for example, getting homesick, not feeling accepted, misunderstandings, etc. Yet, on the plus side, we were also told that in years to come we would probably only remember all the good things, such as the kindness of the host parents, the friendships forged and the language skills gained. (This was indeed true in my case.)

And in my opinion, this is very often the case. Personally, I tend to recall more positive experiences, conversations, or events than bad ones. But maybe I just repress the bad experiences – who knows?

Either way, I tend to remember things in a very positive light. But I know it's all the negative experiences I've had in the course of my life that have also made me who I am today. I have learned some valuable lessons along the way and it's that knowledge I draw on for any subsequent decision-making.

In one of my courses recently, I had a great conversation about the wisdom that comes with age and how wonderful it is not to have to make all the mistakes yourself. Conversations with other people often provide us with the opportunity to learn from their wealth of experience in some way. We don't all have to touch a hot cooker to know that it will hurt. Quite often, all we need is for a person we trust to pass this knowledge on to us.

In fact, I feel truly blessed that I've met so many different people in my life, be it on courses, at presentations, clubs, choir, school, university, kindergarten, in the neighborhood or local community.

Almost every year, I travel to the United Kingdom with my English Club to spend a week discovering a new corner of this beautiful country. But that's only one small aspect of what makes these trips so unforgettable and incredibly valuable to me. One of the biggest joys are the conversations I have with my fellow travelers. They're just brilliant. We like to take our time to have a leisurely breakfast and dinner, sometimes sitting at the table and talking for hours on end. We talk about the past, the here and now, and the future. Some of my friends are fifty years older than me. You can imagine how much greater their wealth of experience is compared to mine. I'm so grateful that they share this with me, allowing me to learn and grow without having to make all the same mistakes that they've made or experience all the fallout from these first-hand.

But I'm also happy to pass on my knowledge, because it gives me the chance to look back on what I've experienced and reflect on it again – and maybe learn something new from it.

Experience is important so that we can grow, whether positive or negative. And if something happens that makes you feel bad, do as my dad always tells me: just chalk it up to experience!

Exercise:

Be open to the experience of others. Be willing to learn from other people's mistakes – that will save you a lot of time. When people in your life tell you stories, be inquisitive, learn as much as you can and then see if you can apply any lessons to your own life. Be grateful for the experience they have 'gifted' to you.

Exercise:

Take care of yourself, lovely – you are so worth it!!! Until next week,

Mandy

You can chalk it up to experience.

Arno Gummerlich

Letter 34

Hi lovely,

Yesterday evening, I had a really enjoyable phone call with my aunt. In fact, I'm still feeling energized from it now. Do you know that feeling too? When you find yourself still drawing inspiration and motivation from a conversation you had with someone days later? That's definitely what happens to me. I always experience an enormous sense of well-being and feel like I've received the best gift ever. It's a bit like the feeling I had as a child after birthdays when I thought about all those lovely presents I'd been given. And if I really think about it, such an interesting and informative conversation, like the one with my aunt, truly is a wonderful gift.

Believe it or not, we were actually talking about work. This might not seem like the most amazing topic in the world – so let me set the scene first.

I come from a family with a very strong work ethic – something I'm incredibly proud of. If any of us say, 'you can rely on me!' then that's exactly what is meant. If you ask one of us to do something, then it will be done – but not in a "that'll do" kind of way; more than likely it will be done better than you expected.

Does that mean a lot of work? Of course, it does! Do we do it gladly? Absolutely! Are we doing it to show off our skills?

No! We do it to make you happy because you are important to us.

For example, if my husband has gone to the workshop early in the morning and I know that he hasn't had breakfast yet, I prepare him a plate full of little treats with things like sliced apple, cheese cubes, grapes, bread, nuts, etc., before delivering it to him in the workshop with a friendly smile. He's always genuinely happy and appreciates the gesture. Obviously, I could just leave it – after all, he's an adult and perfectly capable of learning to organize his own snacks. But then that would mean a serious case of negative thinking and I don't want that. He's my husband and I love him very much. His health and well-being are very important to me which is why I make him the plate of food in the first place. By the same token, my husband sometimes works all night so he can provide for our family. We are all one team, if you will. Each of us uses our various skills to make each other's lives better.

My parents often worked through the night to give us a good life – not only in the form of piano lessons or painting classes, but also to make sure we had fantastic birthdays. My mum often worked late into the night decorating the table for our birthday parties. There was always a place setting with a name tag, serviette ring and then there was the invite itself. I'll never forget the year that all the kids I'd invited rang up to ask what it said in the invitation. They didn't want to open them because they looked so lovely; my mum had made pink cards written in gold with glittery edges wrapped in cellophane and tied up with a beautiful bow. Each card was a work of art. My mum has always had fun decorating and has always gone the extra mile.

When I used to work for other people as an employee, I was always fully committed to working hard and to my best abilities. I used to pretend that the companies were mine, which meant never using up resources unnecessarily and always endeavoring to work with the company's best interests in mind. For example, on business trips I would often take the bus to and from the airport instead of a taxi. Obviously, my boss would have paid for the taxi, but I always thought that it was better to save the money and use it for other things. That's what I do in my own company now, too.

Which brings me back to the conversation with my aunt. It was about working methods, work input and the attitude of employees.

We both feel strongly that it pays to be thoughtful and attentive; for example, the rubbish bag we empty when it's full, even if it's not explicitly stated in our employment contract. Or the job we finish properly, even if the workday is already over – so we don't burden our colleagues with extra work. To us, this means taking full responsibility, being considerate and not forgetting that we have to earn our position. That certainly wouldn't be the case if we created more expense and work than actually being of benefit.

Life is, after all, a constant give and take. Needless to say, there are enough people who always take more than they give. And, yes, that can annoy me sometimes too, but then I always think to myself, do I want to be like these people? The answer is a clear NO.

But you know what? There will always be people like you and me, who get involved, who always do that little bit extra to make the world a better place, and I raise my glass to that. Cheers!

Exercise:

If you find yourself being annoyed by someone who is doing their job strictly by the book, perhaps causing others more work or grief, take a deep breath and be thankful that you can be a wonderful and helpful person who makes the world a little better.

Take care of yourself, lovely – you are so worth it!!! Until next week,

Mandy

Optimists take action, pessimists make excuses.

Marion Gitzel

Letter 35

Hi lovely,

Today, we had another company meeting on the move – I love these "walking meetings"! Have I ever told you about them?

Instead of sitting in a conference room, we go to the forest to walk and talk. This has several benefits. We enjoy being out in the fresh air and being active – unfortunately, something that often falls by the wayside in our everyday life. When we walk, we release endorphins that stimulate our creative juices, so we often come back from the forest positively brimming with ideas and solutions. What's more, we're really happy that we've managed to get our stint of exercise in during working hours. (If only I'd thought of this when I was still at school – it might just have saved me a few of those fail grades in maths … ;-))

This kind of problem solving or – to put it more positively – solution finding, doesn't only apply to work. Going for a walk with my husband, with the children or with friends has also helped to resolve a lot of disagreements and issues.

A walk on your own is also highly recommended to help you clear your head.

I recently introduced the concept of the "walking meeting" to a friend of mine as an alternative to the weekly meetings in her company, as she was telling me how annoyed she gets by how long they last. Not only that, but the room always smells pretty bad and nothing constructive ever seems to get done. In the end, everyone goes back to their desks feeling frustrated and dissatisfied.

Exercise:

Have the courage to take a path you wouldn't do usually; it might just take you somewhere extraordinary. If you are stopped by your own fear, tell yourself that whatever might happen, you still love and accept yourself. Remember the most important relationship that you have is the one with yourself!

Take care of yourself, lovely – you are so worth it!!! Until next week,

Mandy

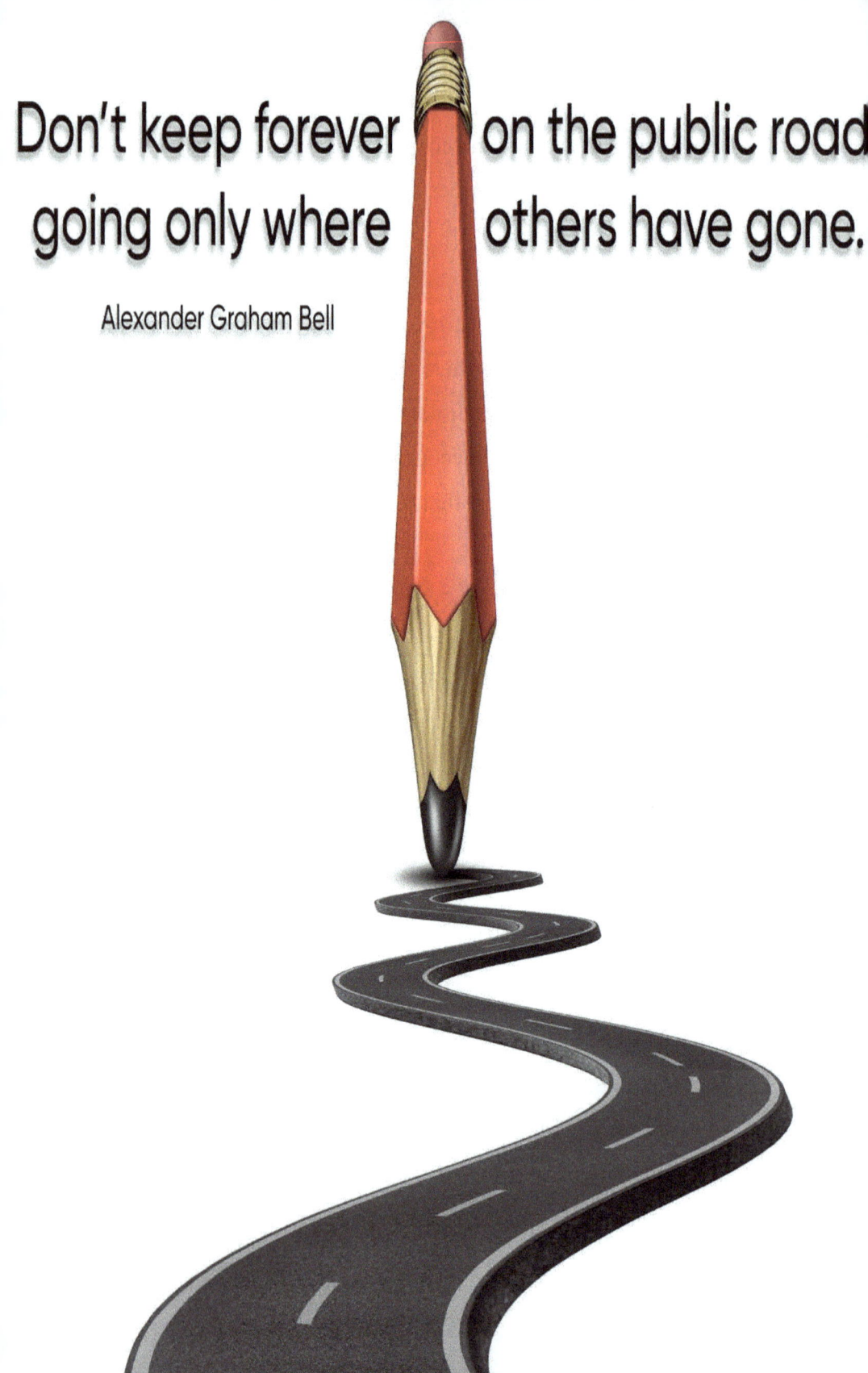

Letter 36

Hi lovely,

The other day, I was listening to the audiobook "The Success Principles" by Jack Canfield when I heard a very interesting idea that really got me thinking.

It involved the following example as told by Jack:

You apply to Harvard University but receive a letter of rejection. However, your life hasn't changed for the worse, it's remained the same. You weren't at Harvard before and you're not going in future. In other words, there's been no actual change in your situation. And you can deal with that, because you haven't attended Harvard at any point in your life to date, and you've still survived anyway.

The second example he described was someone turning down a date. If someone says no, your life is no worse than before, the situation is the same.

I honestly had to think about it for quite a while, because my feelings told me otherwise. My gut told me that if I got a rejection it would make my life worse.

But the longer I spent contemplating these examples, the clearer the picture became – and Jack was of course right.

How can my situation worsen from one second to the next, if nothing has fundamentally changed?

So once again the issue is about how we react to something – in this case, a rejection and how we then deal with that rejection. If we interpret such a situation to mean things like 'I'm worthless, not enough, stupid, not beautiful enough, not lovable', we can't fail but to make ourselves feel bad. But nobody actually said those things – we just tell ourselves that. But why do we do that? We are beautiful, valuable, kind and clever. We know that, or at least we should know that by now! So why would a rejection cause us to have such negative feelings?

Look at it this way: someone somewhere, sometime, will say yes to us, and that someone will be the one who is best for us.

Not every job we may have taken is the right one for us. The next one may be even more suitable and if we had the choice between the two, we would never have taken the first one.

Do you see where this is going? It's all about our point of view, our attitude.

My best friend also provided me with a good example. She was on holiday with her parents and her sister. She and her sister decided to go shopping on their own one afternoon. Their mother was a bit disappointed by that. But then my friend explained to her that it wasn't about choosing her sister over her mum, so the mum had no reason to feel somehow unwanted or unloved.

Do you know the "four-sides" or "four-ears" model of communication?

According to this model, every message has four facets:

1. Factual information
2. Appeal
3. Relationship
4. Self-revelation

For example, the sender of a message may be giving a matter-of-fact statement such as:

"There's no milk left."

However, at that very moment, the receiver may hear that statement with the "relationship ear" turning a simple fact into something like this:

"You weren't paying enough attention again and haven't bought enough milk. So now I'll have to drink my coffee black, which will ruin my whole day. Thanks a lot!"

Do you see what just happened there? The listener has taken their current experiences and feelings and used them to reinterpret the other person's statement into something really negative, when all that was probably meant was, we have to add milk to the shopping list.

I can tell you a thing or two about that, by the way. I listen with the wrong ear far too often. But more about that in the next letter.

I think you're wonderful! (Now, you really can't interpret anything negative into that!)

Exercise:

Which "ear" do you hear with? If you find yourself feeling negative towards something someone has said, ask yourself if it is just a statement of fact after all –instead of your "relationship ear", hear it again with your "factual information" ear! Always assume that people love you and want to do you good, rather than trying to make your life difficult.

Take care of yourself, lovely – you are so worth it!!! Until next week,

Mandy

The fundamental error in thinking is this: The other person thinks like me.

Letter 37

Hi lovely,

This week, I'd like to revisit the subject of last week's letter – communication. I am, after all, the champion of misunderstanding, especially when it comes to communicating with my dear husband. In fact, this is exactly where the miscommunication begins. You may think I'm being ironic about the "dear husband" bit, but I'm not. He is indeed a dear man and sometimes I simply can't understand why I hear his words but understand something completely different to what he's actually saying – and often that means I hear something negative, even though I know that he loves me and only has my best interests at heart.

Since I'm constantly on a drive to improve in all areas of my life, I asked my husband if he would go to a marriage counselling seminar with me. He agreed: 'If it's important to you, I'd be more than happy to.' Great! So, off we went.

My in-laws agreed to take all three children, so once we'd dropped them off, we set off one Friday afternoon on our own.

We'd told some friends about what we were planning to do and had received very mixed reactions. One of the assumptions was that we were about to separate and therefore needed marriage counselling. Others thought it was great that we were having a weekend away together, just the two of us, so that we could spend some quality time with each other.

Our plan was to turn our "good team" into an "excellent team". After all, it wasn't as if we felt we were facing insurmountable difficulties. But we were and still are well aware that there's always room for improvement in our relationship.

The weekend was really enjoyable. We listened to some fantastic presentations, had some intense discussions, went for wonderful walks and slept through every night! We were served breakfast, lunch, coffee and dinner and didn't have to worry about anything but ourselves.

As my husband so aptly pointed out, it was like when we first started out in our relationship, when the only thing we needed to focus on was each other. When a family starts growing, it feels like we increasingly have to divvy up that 100% attention for our partner into more and more areas; for example, we need to focus on our children or on our careers so we can do our jobs properly and provide for the family, not to mention other key areas in life that require our attention.

Anyway, let's return to the weekend seminar I was telling you about. One of the subjects of the presentations was about the partner's family background and upbringing, which really helped us to develop a deeper awareness and understanding of our partner's thought processes and character. Another topic was sex and sensuality, which left us more than relieved to discover that other couples with children felt the same way we did. It's good to know you're not alone. As for the "The 5 Love Languages" (based on the book by Gary Chapman), this was something we were already familiar with, but it was interesting to hear how other couples deal with the subject.

During the talk about communication and the play that was performed to accompany it, my husband and I just looked at each other and grinned; it was as if we were standing on stage ourselves.

At a retreat like this, it goes without saying that solutions are also offered. One communication aid that really impressed us and that we used a lot during that weekend was a small booklet that we both received a copy of. This contained questions we each had to answer; we were to use it to write down our feelings, too, and then at the end of the day swap it with our partner's to read on our own. The great advantage of this booklet and reading it alone was that we had time to think. It also meant we weren't able to express any objections or contest what they'd written along the lines of 'That's not true. That's not what I meant.'

It was incredibly interesting to read how your partner interprets things differently – it was so informative! We certainly learned a lot.

My husband and I agreed that if we had gone to this seminar earlier, we could have saved ourselves a lot of arguments due to lack of awareness and miscommunication.

After all, there's a good reason why they say: communication is the key to success.

Exercise:

The next time you find yourself quarrelling, try to step back for a few minutes to think about what has been said before answering. Ask yourself if what you heard was really what the other person meant. This can save you a lot of frustration and sadness and help you to clear up any misunderstandings for better communication and harmony with your loved one. Take care of yourself, lovely – you are so worth it!!! Until next week,

Mandy

We have two ears and one mouth so that we can listen twice as much as we speak

Epictetus

Letter 38

Hi lovely,

Don't you just love Sundays? No deadline pressure and nowhere to go shopping, at least not where I live.

When I lived in Wales, it was a different story. I even worked in the supermarket on Sundays. For me as a student that was obviously brilliant, because it meant I didn't have to take the late shift after university, but had the early shift for once. But I always wondered why so many people went shopping on Sundays with screaming kids in tow instead of doing something lovely together and focusing on the family as a whole. For me, Sundays were and still are sacred. Nobody goes to work, everyone's at home and we spend the day together as a family.

When I think back to my childhood, it was an amazing time. In the summer, we used to go on bike rides and have picnics, go to the outdoor swimming pool, go boating or visit grandma and grandpa and eat some cake. In the winter, we went sledging and ice skating, played games and made things.

Today, I look at our children and wonder what they will say at some point in the future. 'All you ever did was grumble! We couldn't do anything right!' Isn't that a horrible thought? True, we parents do complain a lot – at least that's how our kids interpret it; we prefer to call it parenting ;-)

Needless to say, my parents were not above a bit of nagging and grumbling either, but I don't really remember it being that bad. Instead, I recall all the lovely things we did. I'm pretty sure there were certain phases when we were growing up, especially during adolescence, where everything was "boring", but luckily, I seem to have forgotten those. What I do remember is my dad taking me to a dyke during a storm surge, and how my mum always made birthdays the highlight of the year.

Lovingly decorated party tables are something that my sister and I still value very much today. In our eyes, birthdays are a way to show our dearest ones just how much we love them. And by that I don't mean the number of presents, but how we decorate the table with colorful sweets, hang up the garlands and bake a cake at five in the morning so that the house smells enticingly good afterwards. Obviously, singing the obligatory Happy Birthday song is also an important part of the occasion.

My own wonderful memories are an incentive for me to make family life as exciting and varied as possible so that we as a family can make many of our own happy memories that the children will enjoy remembering later as adults; for example, our movie nights on a Friday or walks in the forest in the winter wonderland followed by a comforting hot chocolate. Or those evenings spent playing card games by candlelight with plenty of treats on hand. Snuggling up in bed and the countless books that my husband and I read to the children.

Of course, being a parent isn't always that easy. Just when you think everything is going well something comes along to make you feel like a clueless idiot. But it is important to learn to deal with that. Sometimes a low mood or your own problems mean that you start to treat others unfairly. I'm particularly good at that. I'd be lying if I claimed that I'm always well-balanced, level-headed and always manage to keep my composure – I can just hear the kids laughing right now ... But I do endeavor to keep my calm and be more relaxed in such situations, and to always treasure and appreciate my family.

The way I see it, it's up to us to avoid turning on the TV on Sundays or to just let everyone hang out on their own in their rooms, and much better to bring the family together as a unit and create beautiful memories. And Sunday is the perfect day for that. And the great thing is that we all enjoy it so much.

Exercise:

Just give it a go and try and prioritize family life. Go for a walk, spend the afternoon playing games, read aloud by candlelight together. The possibilities are endless. It's over to you.

Take care of yourself, lovely – you are so worth it!!! Until next week,

Mandy

You can't teach children to behave better by making them feel worse. When children feel better, they behave better.

Pam Leo

Letter 39

Hi lovely,

Today, I did something very out of the ordinary. I handed out cake. It may not sound so unusual at first, but the reason certainly is. Today, we learned that our friend's grown-up daughter is terminally ill with cancer. At the moment she is doing well, but since the cancer has progressed so far that chemotherapy would only be able to halt it temporarily, but not beat it, she has decided not to go through with it. She has decided to enjoy the time that she has left without the pain. We also found out that a 24-year-old relative has died, leaving behind a 3-year-old child.

You may well ask where cake comes into this? Well, it's quite simple. We decided we should celebrate life and that means enjoying chocolate cup cakes with gooey centers (and who cares about the calories). Today, we talked a lot about death, about what comes after that, how the bereaved are and how they deal with the loss.

It's always indescribably difficult to lose someone or to watch a loved one pass away, and it seems that no words, no matter how well-intentioned, can bring any comfort.

We discussed the fact that nobody knows how much time they have left. The young woman who decided not to have chemotherapy was told that she now has one to three years to live.

I wonder what I would do with information like that. Of course, I know that we're all going to die at some point, but as we can't know the exact date and time, it all seems so far away and almost unreal.

My immediate thought is to take out a loan and finally do all the things I've always wanted to do, because if I don't do them now, I never will.

I'm still feeling very moved by the opportunity or urgency that presented itself to me today. I've been reminded once again just how important it is to enjoy life to the full every day – to laugh, to love and to forgive and never to hold any grudges.

Life is beautiful, especially in the everyday little things that we so often overlook, wrapped up as we are in our busy, stressful lives.

I always take time for the people I love, because that's what really living means to me. It's all about the wonderful feelings and beautiful sentiments that make up my life. I might be in the middle of an important job, but if my husband needs me for something or one of my kids, even if only to proudly show me their latest Lego tower creation, I take a short breath, try not to get annoyed about the interruption, but be happy and grateful to have this precious moment with my loved ones. The thought that at some point they might not be there anymore and that I would rather work than take time for them is unacceptable to me.

And to ensure that I never get into a situation where I think, 'Oh, if only I had...,' I make the greatest effort every day to be mindful and aware of the people around me and always treat them with the greatest respect and love.

<u>Exercise</u>:

Don't let yourself get annoyed. Life is too precious for bad feelings and moods. Luckily, a thought is just a thought and can be changed if you choose. So, for example, next time you feel annoyed when someone interrupts you, take a deep breath and try to see the bigger picture. Focus on how people enrich your life. Live every day to the full with your loved ones. Remember – love, laugh, forgive and never bear grudges.

Take care of yourself, lovely – you are so worth it!!! Until next week,

Mandy

Were it not for death,
no one would value life.

Jakob Boßhart

Letter 40

Hi lovely,

I realize the last letter was a little heavy so I just want to take the opportunity now to tell you how much I care about you, how much I appreciate you and how precious you are. I'm so grateful that you are part of my life and that I can support and guide you for a while in your life.

I think we often find ourselves thinking about how great someone is and how much we admire them, but for some reason we rarely ever let them know. We all like to hear that we are loved, that we mean the world to someone. So why do we find it so difficult to pay compliments?

When I was younger, I spent a year at a high school in Texas where I found it was common practice to compliment all kinds of people. At the beginning, I found it really disconcerting when someone said to me: 'Wow, your hair looks amazing!' or 'That outfit really suits you!'

As a northern German, I certainly wasn't used to this kind of behavior, but I can't say that I didn't like it! But you know what I like even more than receiving compliments myself? I love paying them. It gives me so much pleasure to make others happy and it always makes me feel like I get a lot back in return.

One evening in the summer, I was out with a friend. We decided we would ride to the harbor on our bikes. As it happened, the outing provided two great opportunities to share some lovely positivity.

The first encounter was with a lady in a beautiful stylish summer dress out with her male companion. As we were parking our bikes, the couple just happened to stroll past. I couldn't help but comment, 'Wow! You look really stunning in that dress!' At first, she looked at me in surprise, then smiled and thanked me. Her companion responded with, 'Yes, I think so too which is why I bought it for her.' She looked radiant and now even more so because a complete stranger had noticed and commented on it. Let's be honest, it's silly not to voice compliments you may be thinking in your head – that's just a waste and nobody gains anything.

The second encounter was with an old biker who I'd noticed a few hours before because of his brightly colored attire and how relaxed he looked on his motorbike. As I passed him, now out and about without his bike, I said, 'I noticed you before. You radiate so much zest for life. I think that's fantastic!' He just grinned at me. My companion said, 'You really know how to make people smile.'

I really do love it! It makes me so incredibly happy. It's my small way of making the world a better place.

It doesn't always have to be compliments either. I recently asked a lady outside the supermarket if everything was all right. She just seemed so sad. She was a little puzzled at first, but then she smiled. She explained that she was just thinking, but that her husband had also mentioned how sad she looked when she was lost in her thoughts. Then she thanked me for showing her compassion.

I can relate, I look pretty aggressive when I'm lost in thought, which is probably why people tend not to disturb me when I'm thinking ;-)

Anyway, to go back to smiling again – it makes life so much easier and so much more enjoyable.

My husband always says that too. When he's not in the best of moods, he simply forces himself to smile and then his mood brightens up all by itself. He does the same thing when stuck in traffic – but I actually think he's more likely to be thinking, 'Smile, you can't kill them all!' ;-)

Exercise:

If you get out of the wrong side of bed in the morning and find yourself in a bad mood, go and stand in front of the mirror and smile at yourself for a minute. You will soon see that it makes you feel better.

Take care of yourself, lovely – you are so worth it!!! Until next week,

Mandy

The most beautiful thing a person can leave behind is a smile on the face of the people who think of them.

Letter 41

Hi lovely,

Today, I want to look at something very practical – a block timetable. It's one of the tools I use to work as effectively as possible in both my home and business life.

Do you still remember your school days and the timetables? In my primary school, one lesson was 45 minutes long; later on, at secondary school it was usually double lessons of 90 minutes.

In other words, you concentrated on maths for 90 minutes until the bell rang for the break. Then you focused on English for 90 minutes, etc. The good thing about this system was that in maths you did maths and were hardly likely to suddenly start working on a German essay or finishing off an art project. No, you concentrated solidly for 90 minutes on what was important at that point in time.

Whether at work or working from home, the lines tend to blur between what the top priority is at any given moment and what actually still needs to be done. That's why we often end up with what feels like a puzzle on our hands. We start tackling one piece, only to find ourselves distracted by another one and so it goes on. We flit from one thing to another and in the end, nothing gets done.

Let's take a look at an example schedule for my company:

8.00–8.30 a.m.	Get to work, drink a tea, define blocks
8.30–10.00 a.m.	Block 1
10.00–10.30 a.m.	Break
10.30 a.m.–12.00 p.m.	Block 2
12.00–1.00 p.m.	Lunch
1.00–2.30 p.m.	Block 3 "walking and talking" meeting in the woods
2.30–2.40 p.m.	Tea break
2.40–4.10 p.m.	Block 4

At first glance, it may seem that we spend more time having breaks than working, but that's definitely not the case. We always try to include four blocks of 90 minutes each, in which we concentrate solely on ONE task. We always have one block which we work through, if possible, whilst walking in the woods. This is where we get creative – for example, we might try and find a subject for a new book or play out various scenarios for a particular problem to find a solution.

The advantage of our 90-minute blocks is that we only have to concentrate on the subject in question. Other topics that still need to be discussed or worked on also have a dedicated block. Nothing is forgotten, everything is dealt with at the appropriate time. It's important that we prioritize the work to be done when we define the blocks. From our point of view, it's also essential to plan in 'downtime' for when we arrive at the office and have our tea, because that also makes for a good work environment. We can still talk and catch up on private matters without losing effective working time.

In our experience, 90-minute blocks are better than 60 minutes, which is often too short. If we finish before the 90 minutes are over, we reward ourselves with another break to recharge our batteries. Obviously, we could start with a new topic, but if we know beforehand that we won't be able to finish it, it will just frustrate us. That's why we go for the break option instead.

I hope I've been able to give you some new ideas. Incidentally, the block timetable is also pretty useful for scheduling other areas of life.

For example:

6.00–7.30 a.m.	Get up, get ready, have breakfast
7.30–8.00 a.m.	Drive to school, childcare, work
8.00 a.m.–12.30 p.m.	Office
12.30–1.00 p.m.	Drive home
1.00–2.00 p.m.	Lunch
2.00–3.00 p.m.	Homework/housework
3.00–4.30 p.m.	Exercise/dates/appointments
4.30–6.00 p.m.	Family time
6.00–7.00 p.m.	Dinner
7.00–7.30 p.m.	Get ready for bed/read a bedtime story/play
7.30–10.00 p.m.	Parent time

In this example, it's not always 90-minute blocks. But then again, family life can't really be compared to office work. I would argue that family organization is much more complex. And a schedule can only be a rough guideline for family life anyway, because something unexpected is bound to happen, and it applies to more than one person. Nevertheless, it can still be a great help to keep track of everything.

Exercise:

Give the time you allocate to yourself, kids or partner the same importance as you would to time set aside for a business meeting or doctor's appointment. Set up a block schedule for your next week and see how much better your concentration is when you know exactly what you need to focus on. It takes some practice, but it will get easier with time.

Take care of yourself, lovely – you are so worth it!!! Until next week,

Mandy

Work expands so as to fill the time available for its completion.

Parkinson's Law

Letter 42

Hi lovely,

Many of my mentors often talk about self-discipline and the fact that it takes a lot of it to stick to a plan.

On the one hand, I certainly get that. If you have a goal in mind, you must never give up and do whatever it takes to achieve it. But on the other hand, I'm also a great admirer of authors like Denise Duffield-Thomas, who uses words like "chillpreneur", i.e. an entrepreneur who is totally chilled about everything.

I love my life and yet I still endeavor to improve myself here and there. My fitness and my weight are always an issue. I have a high degree of self-discipline for a certain period of time, I do a lot of exercise and eat sensibly. Then someone puts a freshly baked loaf of bread and a jar of Nutella in front of me and there go my good intentions. Physical exercise is a subject unto itself. Exercising outside in the summer is no problem at all and I love it, but when it's cold and raining – well, it's probably just best to leave that subject there!

When I'm faced with the choice of chastising myself in order to reach my goal faster, or surrendering to pleasure and then spending a little longer to reach the finishing line, I will quite often go for the indulgence option.

I'm a person who loves life and wants to enjoy it to the max. This means that sometimes, instead of working, I visit a friend or sit in the sun with a cup of tea and just listen to the birds.

Balance is an extremely important word to me. Obviously, I would rather not become overweight any time soon. I wouldn't be able to enjoy my life in the same way if I felt slowed down and sluggish because of my weight. But a couple of kilos aren't going to make that much difference. I basically have a good work ethic and, thanks to my ability to focus, I can do a lot in a short amount of time. But I also have to be careful not to overdo it. The word burnout has definitely come up in my life before and I would like to steer clear of it.

When I manage to create a balance in my life between self-discipline and enjoyment, work and play, a hectic pace and rest, it gives me a tremendous sense of joy and satisfaction.

Obviously, I'm aware of the fact that I can't always just sit back and relax if I really want to finish a project. If I intend to earn a lot of money, I have to do something about it. There's a difference between taking breaks and being lazy or between disciplined work and being a workaholic.

It's often the subtleties in our lives that make the difference. So, when I look at my life and my goals, I choose a path that has set working hours and is interspersed with breaks and wonderful experiences. Another person might choose the path of least resistance and a third person might choose a more punishing one.

Everyone will reach their goal in one way or another, I'm certain of that. However, the state in which we reach the goal depends, as always, on our own decisions.

Exercise:

Choose the path to your goal that's right for you, but don't let others dictate your pace. Try and find a healthy balance between the drive and discipline to fulfil your dreams and taking the time to appreciate and enjoy the journey.

Take care of yourself, lovely – you are so worth it!!! Until next week,

Mandy

The secret of discipline is motivation. When a man is sufficiently motivated, discipline will take care of itself.

Sir Alexander Paterson

Letter 43

Hi lovely,

Do you remember how I was saying last week just how important it is to go your own way and make your own choices? Well, that's what I'd like to take a closer look at this week.

I've often noticed that children like to copy other people a lot. Have you ever noticed that? Suddenly, they seem to turn into mini versions of their parents trying to talk like them or they start imitating a brother or want to dress like a big sister. A few years ago, I was sitting in the organ gallery at church with the choir when the lady next to me said, 'Look, that lad there has grown a beard just like his father's. That shows just how much he admires him.'

When I think about it now, I'm not really sure what to think. So, the son obviously adores his father and wants to emulate him – yet, on the other hand, his father is his own person, we don't need two of him. But we do need a young man with his own mind and personality. We need young people who think for themselves, who develop and contribute to society with their own ideas, not with ideas that may have been around for a long time and may not work anyway.

I have to admit it made me happy when my oldest daughter told me that she'd decorate her flat like mine when she was older (everything symmetrical). I took that as a great compliment. But now I find it so much more wonderful to see how she expresses her personality through her own style. We are all shaped by our parents, the people around us, our environment and other factors. That's why no other person will think exactly the same way as you or I. Admittedly, that can sometimes be quite annoying ;-) But that's also part and parcel of life's rich tapestry – the diverse and exciting world we live in, the reason why we have so many interesting cultures and languages, not to mention all the different ways people have of dealing with life and its challenges.

I don't know the young man in the story above personally, so of course I don't know if he was emulating his father in essence or just thought the beard was cool, but it did get me thinking.

I believe it's very important to honor our roots and the people we love and treat them with respect. But it's equally important to write our own history. We live in a time where any information is just a click away. Knowledge is all-pervading. We have the opportunity to form our own opinions about everything and anything. That means you and I are free to follow trends or create trends of our very own. Everything we need to make well-considered decisions is at our fingertips. But the one thing all the knowledge in the world can't take away from us is actually making a decision and then following it up with action.

There are people who say they can never make up their minds about anything, and yet by not making any decisions, they are in fact making one – to be "indecisive".

So, you see, you never have the option of not deciding – even if you don't act, you have made the decision to do so.

In a sense, this is where we come full circle. Think back to the letter where I told you that no matter what yesterday was like, you have a blank canvas in front of you today and you can just try again. Most decisions can be revised and changed, so don't be afraid to make them.

Exercise:

Have courage and make some decisions! Dream about YOUR perfect life. How would you like to live, where would you like to live, with whom, what would you do all day? Then make a plan of action and finally TAKE one step at a time towards your dream life. You deserve to HAVE IT ALL so dream big, lovely, the world has so much to offer!

Take care of yourself, lovely – you are so worth it!!! Until next week,

Mandy

The biggest mistake, you can make in your life is to be always afraid of making a mistake.

Dietrich Bonhoeffer

Letter 44

Hi lovely,

I visited a dear friend today. We take it in turns to invite each other over for waffles. We talked about the way we have learned to just accept things we can't change.

We talked about relationships with relatives that work better at a distance. Problems in ('patchwork') families that arise when we don't understand each other's ways of thinking, leading to frequent disagreements.

Sometimes life throws obstacles in our way that seem so huge and heavy we would rather go and hide or run away from any responsibility. Reactions like this are normal. We're only human, and we can become overwhelmed. The most important thing is not to be hard on yourself for having the immediate urge to want to escape from it all. I think this is nothing unusual.

Let's say you're pregnant and at the start of a wonderful journey. You feel your body changing and getting ready for the new life growing inside you. Ideally, this journey ends with a healthy child who brings you nothing but joy.

Sometimes, however, the reality is different. Sometimes children are born with disabilities – mental or physical, maybe both. What then? Don't parents have the right to feel overwhelmed at first? Of course, they do! I can imagine that most parents would feel this way at the beginning. The love they feel for their child is not in question. The point I want to make here is more to do with all their dreams and expectations being turned upside down and how this takes an enormous amount of adjustment. They have to reorganize their thoughts and develop a new idea about enjoying family life despite the initial difficulties.

The parents I know who have disabled children felt this way at the beginning. But once they had all come to terms with the unexpected circumstances and their new understanding of each other, now feel overwhelmed – but with love, joy and gratitude.

I also know parents who, having given birth to healthy children, find themselves despairing as soon as these children reach puberty – suddenly, what and who they have known, who they were used to is gone. Everything has changed and is different to their expectations.

Just as in other letters, attitude is key here too. Of course, it sometimes takes a while to say goodbye to our expectations and to the future we have imagined for ourselves. Sometimes this can even feel like mourning, but it is so important to adjust our attitude to one of acceptance.

This can also apply to much more trivial things too, a holiday or a job that doesn't turn out the way you had hoped, for example. You always have two options in this situation:

1. You mope around, don't change anything and are unhappy.

2. You accept the situation as it is, and then dig deep to find a way to make the best of it and create your BEAUTIFUL LIFE.

Once again, it's up to us; who would have thought it? ;-)

<u>Exercise:</u>

Analyze situations in your current life that were unexpected and that may be overwhelming you. The most important thing is not to blame yourself for that initial feeling of wanting to run away – that's quite a normal reaction. But remember it's up to you to decide if you can change the situation or accept it. Try and make the best of an unexpected situation so that you can fill your life with more joy.

Take care of yourself, lovely – you are so worth it!!! Until next week,

Mandy

God, give me the serenity,
to accept the things I cannot change,
the courage to change the things
I can change, and the wisdom,
to distinguish one from the other.

Reinhold Niebuhr

Letter 45

Hi lovely,

I received an e-mail today from a lady in the USA. She was assigned to me as a so-called "accountability partner". This simply means that I have to be accountable to her for my actions.

Maybe that sounds negative at first, but it's not at all. After all, I'm the one who signed up for this. It's a way for me to put pressure on myself to reach my goals faster.

By the way, I'm not new to this. My business partner and I used to be each other's accountability partners, but we found that we were just too nice and understanding of each other.

But when I have to tell a stranger, a businesswoman in the USA, that I missed my deadline (one I set for myself) because I had my period and accompanying stomach and back pain, she'll tell me to get a grip instead of responding with understanding. And that's exactly what I need sometimes. Someone to tell me to my face that I need to stop making excuses and just get on with it.

Reading this now, it does feel a bit like I'm deliberately punishing myself, but it moves me forward without actually doing any harm. It's more about my own guilty conscience kicking in when I know I'm about to get a phone call and I've been watching TV for the last three days rather than sticking to the plan I'd promised. After all, the plan isn't for anyone else but me! And to make sure that my inner procrastinating self doesn't scupper my plan, I look for an "accountability partner" to help me stay on track.

I strongly believe that we don't have to do everything on our own and that we can get help. This is not only true when it comes to the household chores or with a project, it's also true in situations where we might be struggling with ourselves.

I have many friends who see psychologists because sometimes they just need someone who doesn't come from their inner circle and who can offer an objective view about a situation from the outside.

Of course, it also helps to talk to family or friends or to have a good laugh, but when we feel like we're banging our heads against a wall and family or friends mean well but can't help us, then it's time for an outsider.

Marriage counsellors, for example, are always a good idea when the same problem keeps coming up in a marriage. My husband and I went to a marriage coaching session once and it got us so much further than we ever thought possible after just one session. Needless to say, we had tried to solve the issue on our own first, but somehow, we got stuck and since we both wanted to resolve the issue, we looked for an outside person who could help us find a solution together. We would probably never have come up with the ideas she gave us on our own, or perhaps only much later on. She led us to unexpected solutions by asking simple questions; it was great.

I see the following image in my mind's eye: two people walking from different directions towards a crossing, both armed with road maps and yet unsure of where to go from there. High above them, an eagle circles, keeping an eye on all the roads for miles around. In this scenario, the eagle would be the outsider who can offer different solutions because of its different perspective.

Exercise:

Sometimes it takes a lot of effort to ask for help because we're afraid that it will be seen as weakness. But essentially, it shows our wisdom. So, dare to ask for help or to accept help that is offered.

Take care of yourself, lovely – you are so worth it!!! Until next week,

Mandy

Surround yourself with people who help you to make the best of yourself.

Letter 46

Hi lovely,

I had a bit of spare time to watch a YouTube video during a tea break today. It was a video from Jordan Page (the 'Fun, Cheap or Free Queen', a blogger from America). Made earlier this year, she had been travelling a lot with her family during the holidays while workmen were in the house. The house looked like a bomb had hit it. She made no secret of the fact that she felt totally overwhelmed by the situation. She usually has her family, household and herself under control, but this time it was all too much for her.

I think we've all been there. Sometimes we feel we're getting left behind, we can't keep up with housework, we might get sick and domestic chaos takes over.

But what I find particularly likeable about Jordan is that she doesn't hide such "shortcomings" by pretending to be perfect.

And she said something that made me laugh. She said 'Everybody loves a train wreck. I have no problem being the train wreck.' I hadn't heard that saying before, but I knew immediately what she meant.

After all, we're all secretly happy when we see others having the exact same struggles we do. Be it the screaming child in the supermarket, the domestic chaos when we try to become masters of our own laundry, or the burnt food because we tried to do everything at once. When we see these things happening to others, we get a sense of relief because it means we're not the only ones who experience it.

I'm thinking of a really funny situation right now, actually two that happened to me.

One time, as mentioned in previous letters, I was clearing out my house using the KonMari method. During the process, downstairs looked like a battlefield. Bags, boxes, and loose items were strewn everywhere; we could barely move. Then one morning, a friend of ours came to visit. He came into the hallway, greeted us, stared at the mess, and asked if he could take a picture. Then he laughed. He said, 'I'm so happy to see this mess. My wife and I always feel so disorganized and untidy when we compare ourselves to you, and now this! It's good to see that you have chaotic days too; that makes me feel much better!' That was unexpected! Not only was I not even aware that others were comparing themselves to me (which is a dumb idea, by the way, to compare yourself to anyone), I felt like I was helping someone, thanks to my mess.

The other time, we were sitting in my dining room having tea when someone said, 'That's brilliant! Mandy, look at your TV cabinet; it's all dusty.'

I replied with a grin, 'First of all, you should be ashamed of yourself for getting so excited about other people's dust. And secondly, that's not dust at all, the granite slab always looks like that.'

The guy actually got up and wiped his finger across the granite slab to check it wasn't dust. It wasn't, he was disappointed. Honestly, if I'd known beforehand how much pleasure people would get from my place being neither tidy nor dust-free, I could have saved myself a lot of cleaning stress.

Exercise:

Make people happy by showing that you, too, are human.

Take care of yourself, lovely – you are so worth it!!! Until next week,

Mandy

As long as humanity connects us, it doesn't matter what separates us.

Finnish saying

Letter 47

Hi lovely,

The other day I got my hands on my old dictionary. It looked pretty battered. But then again, I did give it a good run for its money during all those years of studying. I smile when I think about how I spent nights poring over a translation and translating texts with the help of my trusty dictionary. I always loved studying, especially at night when the house was quiet.

Today I still love to learn, but now I sleep at night. My whole daily routine and my whole rhythm have changed a lot since my years studying. I used to love working through the night and proudly submitting a paper the next day.

But that's how life and times change. I still love to study today, as I said, but I've had to find a way to incorporate it into my life. When I'm on holiday, I love to read books, which I do during the day. I just can't manage it in the evenings. But I also wanted to find a way to incorporate books into my life when I wasn't on holiday. So, I started with audiobooks. They're brilliant to listen to on the train, in the car or while cooking. In the beginning it was CDs, but now I use my phone.

For me, audiobooks are always a little excursion into another world. I used to listen to a lot of historical novels or the latest bestsellers. Nowadays, I listen to a lot of books about personal development. Since I'm fluent in English, I'm lucky enough to have a range of English and German audiobooks to choose from. I'm always happy when I drop my little one off at kindergarten in the morning and can then switch from "Bob the Builder" to my audiobook. That's a little more me-time. I often have a delicious tea in my thermal mug and so the otherwise dull drive to work, or even back again, becomes a little relaxing break where I learn something.

I have always been inquisitive. When I travelled to China, the immersion into an unfamiliar world was incredibly fascinating.

Thanks to audiobooks, I can now delve into fascinating ideas and impressions at the touch of a button in my car or in the kitchen. I'm glad that when I graduated, I didn't just say 'Thank goodness the learning is over.' I realized that life is one big school where we take a whole host of subjects at a wide variety of times. My major at the moment is "Wife and Mother". My minor is "Businesswoman". All the minor courses I take on the side include "Nutrition", "Dispute Management", "Gardening", "Hospitality" and many more besides.

And every subject is fun because it's more obvious to me now than ever before: I'm learning for me and for MY life, not for anyone else.

I've had to get out of the classroom, away from books, into audiobooks, and into real life, but it has been worth leaving the familiar path to try something new.

<u>Exercise</u>:

Think of your life as your own personal school: Which subjects would you choose? Where would go on your class trips? What would you like to learn?

Take care of yourself, lovely – you are so worth it!!! Until next week,

Mandy

You can never dress too well
or
be too well educated.

Oscar Wilde

Letter 48

Hi lovely,

Today, I spent a magical afternoon on a coffee date with some wonderful friends. Everyone there was a current or previous member of the English Club. We talked about all the wonderful trips we've made together and how funny it is that such close friendships have developed over the years. Most of my students would never have met if I hadn't had the courage to simply put an ad in the newspaper all those years ago. At the time, I wanted to start an English Club and was looking for people interested in joining me.

Looking around the group was really heart-warming. I was responsible for bringing all these people together. I was the one who had taken them all on a journey. Me! I was filled with a true sense of pride, because I'd taken action and set something wonderful in motion.

This is what I keep trying to tell you: You have to act if you want to make a difference!

In this case, it was as easy as a phone call to the newspaper. I still can't quite believe what has grown out of that "go on, just be brave for 5 seconds and actually pick up the phone and dial the number" moment. I could shed a tear I'm so moved right now. And I'm not saying this to tell you how fantastic I am. Rather it's about convincing you that you too can achieve wonderful things.

I used to marvel at women and men who were able to create an impact, who inspired and carried people with them. And I always thought, 'Oh, if only I were someone like that, who had the ability to do great things.' But I had yet to learn that "great" is often found in small things.

If I think about it now, I've already done or accomplished so many of the things that I dreamed of when I was a child.

I was an exchange student in the USA for a year, I have been a host mother for three children from Belarus and soon from other countries too. I have travelled half the world, studied abroad and started my own company. I've organized glittering parties and wonderful trips. And how has all this been possible? I just did it. So simple! I made a decision and then I did everything necessary to reach my goal. Has it been complicated? Difficult? Absolutely! And sometimes very exhausting, but in retrospect all the effort has definitely been worthwhile.

And today I feel a deep sense of pride because I dared to take the plunge.

Do you remember my first letter? I could give my former self a big fat kiss because she put so much effort into my/our future.

Exercise:

Take the plunge and start to realize your dreams. I've given you lots of tools in my letters, now it is up to you to use them and start living your best life!

Take care of yourself, lovely – you are so worth it!!! Until next week,

Mandy

He who takes the plunge
into cold water,
dives into a sea
of possibilities.

Finnish saying

Letter 49

Hi lovely,

Today, I would like to tell you something about perseverance. In my letters, I've often encouraged you to just get on and start something and that the path to success lies through action. And very briefly, I've also talked about perseverance.

I owe a few of my own success stories to perseverance.

One example: "Guest: Mandy Ekat" becomes

"Candidate: Mandy Ekat".

When I received the e-mail with the agenda and saw that I was no longer listed as a "guest" but as a "candidate", I was overjoyed.

I'm working towards being accepted into an international association that promotes women and education around the world. Before I can be accepted, I first have to prove that I will be a valuable member. This takes months and can be pretty nerve-wracking; after all, who likes to hear that they don't make the grade? But I'm confident that my status will change to "member" soon enough, because I'm going to give it my best shot. And even though my end goal has not yet been fully realized, I'm nevertheless happy to have this first step of becoming a candidate under my belt. There had been a moment when I thought I'd made it to "member" status, but one person still needed convincing. So, it was time to persevere with my work and show that I'm worthy.

The club evenings I was invited to as a candidate and where I could show what I had to offer, have resulted in other people becoming aware of me and have led to further invitations, to expert round tables, for example. This wouldn't have happened if I hadn't persevered, always given my best and persisted with my bid to join the association.

It's so important that we always try to do our best because we never know who is watching or listening. Doors open unexpectedly when we are fully engaged.

If I had given up just because I didn't make it on the first attempt, I would have missed all the opportunities that came by persevering.

Exercise:

Be persistent in everything you do. Always do your best and persevere, so you never have to feel bad about letting yourself down.

Take care of yourself, lovely – you are so worth it!!! Until next week,

Mandy

What takes time, will be worth it in the end.

German proverb

Letter 50

Hi lovely,

In these letters, I've introduced you to many methods and given you ideas that I hope encourage you to get the best out of yourself. My intention has never been to suggest that you are not enough. No, quite the contrary! I pass on this information with love and I know what great potential lies in wait within you. I know that you can turn "good" into "great" and that you can make your beautiful life even more fantastic.

You are wonderful just the way you are. You create your life following your own aspirations, and yet I'm sure there are moments in your life, as in mine, that give you cause to stop and wonder if you are still doing the right thing. Are you still heading towards your goal or have you gone off course?

One area where I often find this is with my weight and therefore my health. If I pay attention to all the little things like "drinking enough water", "eating a balanced diet" and "getting enough exercise" and really do them, everything is in balance. But if I let myself go and eat more bread with Nutella than fruit and vegetables or lie on the couch more than getting out for some exercise in the fresh air, I notice it and not just because my trousers are tight. I also notice it in my bad skin and how dissatisfied I feel in myself.

Do you know what the annoying thing is? It really is just down to the little things. So, what's easy to do is also easy not to do, and that's the crux of the whole thing.

Because if I lose sight of my goal, in this case a healthy lifestyle, then it becomes easy to indulge in pleasure, and more than just occasionally (which would be OK).

So, when this happens and I notice I'm off course what do I do? First of all, I recommit to my goal of a healthy lifestyle and remind myself of the reasons why I've chosen to live like this – for example, more mobility, more energy, and a healthier appearance. Then I take stock of my environment. I need to make sure that I make it as easy as possible to live healthily. For example, by removing all of the unhealthy food from my fridge and cupboards and only buying food that is in line with my goal.

At the same time, I need to make it as difficult as possible to fall back into the old habits that I'm trying to change.

I once heard a really funny idea. It related to a person who was constantly overspending. Of course, this wasn't about spending money on food or everyday necessities, but on luxury items. A coach advised the person to freeze their credit cards in a block of ice. The idea being it would be very difficult to make an impulse purchase. The person would have to wait for their credit card to defrost, and by then, the impulse to spend money would hopefully have passed.

It's important to realize that it's the simple things that are often very difficult. But WE can make them happen by focusing on them and by taking 100% responsibility.

Exercise:

Find ways to make it as easy as possible for you to reach your goals.

Take care of yourself, lovely – you are so worth it!!! Until next week,

Mandy

It is so easy to convince others;
It is so difficult to convince oneself.

Letter 51

Hi lovely,

Today I would like to share a poem by Petrus Ceelen with you:

A Gift from Heaven

Some people do not know

How important it is that they are simply there.

Some people do not know

How good it feels just to see them.

Some people do not know

How comforting their kind smile is.

Some people do not know

The sustenance their company brings.

Some people do not know

How much poorer we would be without them.

Some people do not know

That they are a gift from heaven.

They would know if we told them.

(Translated into English by Becky Lange)

I was sent this poem together with a thank you card. I felt so infinitely loved as I read it. Of course, I know that the people around me love and appreciate me, but to actually hear or read it was heart-warming. It made me realize once again how important communication is. I'm going to copy this poem and pass it on, because I want to tell my loved ones how valuable they are to me as well. And I'm also sending it to you.

Feel loved, my lovely!

Exercise:

Tell the people you love and who are important to you how you feel. And more importantly, act with love so that there is no room for doubt.

Take care of yourself, lovely – you are so worth it!!! Until next week,

Mandy

A Gift from Heaven

Some people do not know
how important it is that they are simply there.
Some people do not know
how good it feels just to see them.
Some people do not know
how comforting their kind smile is.
Some people do not know
the sustenance their company brings.
Some people do not know
how much poorer we would be without them.
Some people do not know
that they are a gift from heaven.
They would know if we told them.

Petrus Ceelen

Letter 52

Hi lovely,

So, we have reached the end of our one-year journey. Every week during the past year I have written to you. I'm so infinitely grateful for this opportunity you have given me.

One of my mentors, Jim Rohn, once said, 'When you share your wisdom with ten people, you have the chance to hear your own teachings ten times and internalize them'.

Mike Dooley also said that we teach best what we need to learn ourselves.

By giving me the opportunity to write down my own stories, advice, and wisdom, you have given me the chance to rethink and reapply it all.

I thank you for this with all my heart!

I'm going to stop writing to you for now so that you have the chance to apply your newly acquired knowledge. Think of it as the foundation of a building. You have to let it settle before you can continue with construction.

My mentor, Darren Hardy, believes that it's better to read one book five times than to continually read new ones for five weeks. This doesn't mean, of course, that we should only ever read one book; it simply means that instead of reading books superficially, we should delve deeply into them.

I always find that when I read a book or listen to an audiobook again, I discover new inspiration and ideas to carry into my life.

Exercise:

Dip back into this book and read the letters again. This will be helpful as you begin to use some of the tools I have given you. You can keep in touch with me by going to my website or following me on Instagram (www.Mandyekat.de insert details) where I regularly post my thoughts and ideas about living life to the full and finding your better self.

All my love!

Mandy

The Road Not Taken

Two roads diverged in a yellow wood,
And sorry I could not travel both
And be one traveler, long I stood
And looked down one as far as I could
To where it bent in the undergrowth;

Then took the other, as just as fair,
And having perhaps the better claim,
Because it was grassy and wanted wear;
Though as for that the passing there
Had worn them really about the same,

And both that morning equally lay
In leaves no step had trodden black.
Oh, I kept the first for another day!
Yet knowing how way leads on to way,
I doubted if I should ever come back.

I shall be telling this with a sigh
Somewhere ages and ages hence:
Two roads diverged in a wood, and I—
I took the one less traveled by,
And that has made all the difference.

Robert Frost

Lightning Source UK Ltd.
Milton Keynes UK
UKHW022259280222
399360UK00006B/183